W0050322

100 Ideas for Primary Teachers:

Supporting Pupils with Autism

Francine Brower

BLOOMSBURY EDUCATION

LONDON OXFORD NEW YORK NEW DELHI SYDNEY

BLOOMSBURY EDUCATION
Bloomsbury Publishing Plc
50 Bedford Square, London, WC1B 3DP, UK

BLOOMSBURY, BLOOMSBURY EDUCATION and
the Diana logo are trademarks of Bloomsbury Publishing Plc

First published in Great Britain, 2019 by Bloomsbury Publishing Plc

A catalogue record for this book is available from the British Library

ISBN: PB: 978-1-4729-6157-0; ePDF: 978-1-4729-6156-3;
ePub: 978-1-4729-6155-6

2 4 6 8 10 9 7 5 3 1

Typeset by Newgen KnowledgeWorks Pvt. Ltd., Chennai, India
Printed and bound by CPI Group (UK) Ltd, Croydon, CR0 4YY

To find out more about our authors and books visit
www.bloomsbury.com and sign up for our newsletters

Contents

Acknowledgements

I would be remiss if I did not take this opportunity to offer sincere thanks to all of the colleagues who have inspired me through their creative commitment to supporting children, young people and adults with autism. Many have had an impact on my career through providing encouragement, challenges, opportunities and sound advice. I am so grateful for the opportunity offered to me by Inscape House (formerly a school of Boys and Girls Welfare Society and now The Together Trust), where my journey into the world of autism began over two decades ago. I have known many colleagues, like myself, who became absolutely passionate about learning more and longing for greater understanding in order to support individuals on the autism spectrum, their families and carers. The learning never ceases.

I would like to thank my editor, Chloe Fitzsimmons, for her encouragement, suggestions and availability in responding to my many questions.

Learning, however, is not limited to professional colleagues. It could not occur without the children, young people and adults who have crossed my path. They are the true teachers who enable us to know when we get it right and when we fail and who rely on us to try again, to seek answers and to empower them to have a voice and to succeed, often against the odds.

Through the years of working with individuals with autism, my family has been my constant backdrop. My husband, Kent, has laughed with me, celebrated with me and cried with me. My children and grandchildren have listened to my stories and grown in their own understanding of disability and autism. I am forever grateful for each of them.

Introduction

When Bloomsbury invited me to write a new edition of my book on autism, I accepted the challenge without hesitation. For 25 years my interest in autism and my passion for individuals on the spectrum, their families/carers and the professionals who offer support has continued to grow. I have found that many of my colleagues, like myself, enter the world of autism and make it their life's work, striving to learn more, to improve understanding and insight and to make a difference to those they work with.

The ideas in this book are written with a wide menu of provision in mind – mainstream, resourced, generic special and ASD specialist schools. I want to encourage you to recognise the many and varied positive attributes of children while being realistic about the obstacles to overcome. I encourage you to be creative in problem solving, to demonstrate empathy and warmth while you reach beyond the curriculum per se and nurture self-esteem, confidence, emotional wellbeing and the enjoyment of life.

All children need to be included, and within education this term, 'included', is often associated with being on the register of a mainstream school. But it is wider than that – it is inclusion in the peer group at school, in activities, in the community and in the daily experiences of life. Within this book, the term 'reasonable adjustments' will reference some of these issues.

While understanding has developed a great deal over recent years, there continue to be many unanswered questions about autism. Research is ongoing to confirm cause, genetics, prevalence, improved diagnosis, interventions, etc. It is a frustration that families continue to face a battle for diagnosis, gaps in provision, a lack of high-quality services, exclusions from school and unacceptably high unemployment in adulthood. Everyone involved in the field of autism – individuals with a diagnosis, families and professionals – longs for the day when there is better understanding and infrastructure to meet the unique needs of children and adults with autism.

This book offers information and ideas to support work with children with autism in the primary years. Those of you who take the time to learn, to search for answers, to truly listen to your pupils, their families and your colleagues, can make an amazing difference to the child's quality of life. You can be the catalyst to help recognise strengths and make progress possible. You can reduce anxiety, provide new opportunities, create new interests and open up the world for the child.

I challenge you to work together as colleagues, embracing families and carers, and striving to make your school a welcoming and well-equipped environment to meet the individual needs of children on the autism spectrum. My greatest joy would be that this book would stimulate you to follow up on ideas and unleash your creativity in the classroom. Take this opportunity to recognise and develop your own gifts to meet the needs of this amazing group of children. You may even find that you learn more from them than they do from you!

How to use this book

This book includes quick, easy and practical ideas for you to dip in and out of, to help you to support the pupils in your care and give them the best learning experiences possible.

Each idea includes:

- a catchy title, easy to refer to and share with your colleagues
- an interesting quote linked to the idea
- a summary of the idea in bold, making it easy to flick through the book and identify an idea you want to use at a glance
- a step-by-step guide to implementing the idea.

Each idea also includes one or more of the following:

Teaching tip
Practical tips and advice for how and how not to run the activity or put the idea into practice.

Taking it further
Ideas and advice for how to extend the idea or develop it further.

Bonus idea ★
There are 34 bonus ideas in this book that are extra-exciting, extra-original and extra-interesting.

Online resources also accompany this book. When an online resource is referenced in the book, follow the link www.bloomsbury.com/100-ideas-primary-autism to find extra resources, catalogued under the relevant idea number. Here you can also find the full list of website addresses mentioned in the book.

Share how you use these ideas and find out what other practitioners have done using **#100ideas**.

Understanding
leads to acceptance

Part 1

The spectrum

'I was so confident when Anthony, a pupil with autism, was joining my class. I had worked with Stephen two years earlier so it would be easy, right? Wrong. It was like relearning everything!'

Complex needs, severe learning difficulties, highly intelligent, non-verbal, highly verbal, socially aloof, seeking to be social, profound sensory processing issues, mild sensory issues, highly anxious, placid... The spectrum is wide and can be confusing. Only by recognising the needs of *each* individual can we begin to offer the necessary support.

Teaching tip

You, your attitudes, understanding, training, perseverance, creativity and energy are critical to finding the key to unlocking both the child and the child's own way into the complex world of learning. I have long proclaimed that we do not want children with autism to just cope in our schools. We want them to thrive!

To make the most of the ideas in this book, it is essential that you have a basic overview of the autism spectrum. Every child you meet will be a wonderful, unique character who needs to be accepted, cared for and supported as an individual.

- From the beginning, look for the child's strengths – not just the deficits! It is too easy to be caught up in what the child struggles with, what might challenge you as a teacher or what the problems are. Of course you need this information, but celebrate what the child does well, enjoys and responds to.
- Recognise that early intervention is important in supporting the child to engage, respond and develop internal strategies *but* if the child comes to your school beyond the Early Years, do not assume that you cannot have a very positive impact on their development and learning. Given the right interventions, consistency and creative input, you can have a positive influence on the present and future of the child.

Further information on the breadth of the ASD spectrum can be found in the online resources for this book.

High expectations

'Oh, he can't do anything. He only participates if he likes what we're doing!' (The response from the manager when I asked about the strengths of a child in a nursery setting who was referred to my specialist ASD school)

Don't we all participate better when we enjoy what we're involved in? The very nature of the difficulties related to autism can 'block' learning and lead to assumptions about ability to learn – high expectations are essential to tap into the actual potential of the child.

Never make assumptions about the child's level of ability without ensuring that there has been full assessment of needs. Getting a window into the pupil's strengths and weaknesses, gathering a full profile through family, multi-professional assessment and observation will be the starting point for identifying interventions, teaching and learning styles, motivators and sensory processing issues. The contributors will include:

- parents/carers
- educational psychologist
- speech and language therapist
- clinical psychologist
- occupational therapist
- baseline assessment within school
- prior education reports from Early Years and previous placement.

Every piece of information is necessary to create a full picture and to underpin the emotional wellbeing of the child. The various parts of the mosaic work together and cannot be isolated from each other. Communication and access to learning, sensory and anxiety issues, social interaction, communication and relationships overlap and need to be understood as part of the whole, not in isolation.

Teaching tip

Timely reminders of the successes of the children and visual prompts for staff to maintain high expectations will keep this topic high on the agenda.

Bonus idea ★

Whether your school is mainstream or special, look for an 'autism champion' from within the staff team – a go-to person for support with problem solving, an individual who is supported to access additional training or qualifications and who can effectively cascade learning and share good practice.

Ethos enables

'When we were visiting schools to find the right place for our son with autism it just "felt" right.'

Ethos refers to the character and guiding beliefs that permeate a school, its approach and atmosphere.

Taking it further

A useful grid is available in the online resources to assess your school against these characteristics.

Have you ever walked into a place and felt relaxed and at home? I have! Many such experiences have been in schools, both mainstream and special. It's very difficult to define why, but consider your school in light of these characteristics:

- mutual respect – adult to adult, adult to child, child to adult
- the wellbeing of all at the heart of the school
- positive attitudes – empathy
- emphasising strengths and addressing difficulties
- strong communication within and without
- parents/carers as true partners
- inclusiveness, making reasonable adjustments
- high expectations for everybody
- warm relationships
- rapport
- the use of humour
- group problem solving
- sensitivity and alertness to pupil needs
- celebration of diversity
- willingness to take constructive criticism
- the freedom to ask hard questions without it being a threat
- a culture of always asking 'Why?' when things don't go to plan
- a quiet, purposeful atmosphere
- well-organised space.

Do you recognise this school? Consider using this as a checklist for discussion and seek honest evaluation of where your school fits.

Bonus idea ★

Develop a confidential questionnaire, adding a five-point scale to give you a picture of the ethos of your school, and use the information to develop a plan to address areas of weakness and to celebrate your strengths.

Parents as partners

'I realised that I had missed a valuable asset by not spending more time getting the home and family perspective. Talking things over thoroughly made such a difference in consistency.'

Schools often pay lip service to parents being the expert on their child and too often forge ahead without a full understanding of background, what has been tried before and how sharing and problem solving together can reap benefits for all.

Here are some key points to consider:

- Communication between home and school is essential. It must be regular and have meaning. Many schools continue to use a written home–school diary but parents often express frustration if the daily entry is 'fine' or 'had a good day'. Remember that many children are not able to chat about their day and that parents are keen to be made aware of difficult issues and successes.
- Current technology provides a powerful tool for keeping parents/carers in the picture. Providing photographs of the child's involvement in activities, exposure to new experiences, independent work being done, participation with peers, relaxing, etc. is a concrete way to show progress and positive engagement.
- Be honest in expressing the concerns you have or negative incidents that have arisen and need to be shared, but NEVER let these dominate the communication. Give careful consideration to how you report incidents – a conversation (recorded in a log book) is often more helpful than a written note. Always look for ways to praise the child and build self-esteem.

The online resources offer ideas on relevant training for parents and guardians.

Communication

'I recognised that communication was an issue for some of my pupils but it wasn't until I realised I had to alter the way I communicated that things improved.'

We are so accustomed to talking and expecting that everyone around us can follow our words at speed. We often slow down (and sometimes increase volume) when we are communicating with someone whose first language is not our own. When it comes to our children on the autism spectrum, we need to proactively communicate in specific and appropriate ways.

Teaching tip

Take every opportunity to clearly articulate words relevant to the situation, objects, actions, emotions, etc.

How do we do this? To begin with, we have to have an understanding of what the child's method of communication is and support them with the recommended interventions (see Part 2 for more detail on this).

Here are some strategies to use when communicating with the child with autism:

- Consistency is essential in the words you use and the manner in which they are delivered.
- Key words – 'economy of language' – will help the child to get a clear message that is not lost in lengthy sentences laden with superfluous vocabulary.
- Beware of literal understanding and ensure that your intent is understood, e.g. 'Can you give me a hand?'.
- SLOW DOWN – allow processing time before you rephrase or repeat the instruction.
- Concrete, visual reinforcement through objects, photographs, symbols and/or the written word is important.
- Use a calm, unemotional voice to deliver measured volume.
- Be patient and recognise that your communication can pay dividends over time.

With the support and assessment of a speech and language therapist, identify the stage

of communication: pre-intentional (not yet recognising that communication is shared with others) to verbal.

Once you have this information, set appropriate targets based on the child's current communication and how this will be progressed – this will range from the use of objects of reference, through the use of photographs or symbols, to the written word and verbal communication for both receptive and expressive language. Be aware that some children with autism may not develop verbal communication and will rely on other strategies to enable them to make their needs and opinions known. Be alert to every effort the child makes to gain your attention and to express a need. Use each of these opportunities to affirm the child's effort and help the child to link it to the communication exchange. For example, if the child pulls you to the sink, offer a drink and use the opportunity to emphasise the word drink; use gesture and show a cup. If rejected, offer 'wash hands', again emphasising the vocabulary and demonstrate washing hands. In this way you are communicating what the child may be asking for and building a foundation for future communication and understanding. Ensure that the information and targets are adopted by each individual supporting the child.

Examples of targets:

Receptive language:

- To understand and respond to two key words, clearly delivered and repeated after a ten-second pause (the adult to accompany verbal instruction with photographs to reinforce meaning).

Expressive language:

- To make a request by exchanging a symbol representing a desired object.
- To recognise when a peer wants to join a conversation and pause to listen.

> **Bonus idea**
>
> Agree with colleagues, in advance of any issue, that anyone not adhering to the outlined communication strategy will be reminded to ensure that consistency is achieved.

Your flexible friend

'He insists on doing things in his own way and if I change what we're doing, he just can't cope. It's so frustrating at times!'

Most of us struggle with change and prefer routine and predictability. But when we face change and disappointment, we have coping strategies – ways to accept the unexpected. Given that a desire for sameness is one of the issues faced by most individuals with autism, rigidity is to be expected.

Teaching tip

Use a symbol, such as a surprised face, to highlight changes on the timetable and review them at the start of the day.

Taking it further

Use visuals such as calendars, timetables, Social Stories™ and Comic Strip Conversations to reinforce and encourage acceptance.

Example 1: Lisa wore a watch and was able to tell the time. The timetable said that dinner was at 12.00. Sometimes an activity was running slightly late, with a couple of extra minutes needed to complete it. But at 12.00 sharp, Lisa downed tools! Time to stop. Explaining that it was okay to carry on briefly was difficult for her to accept – but in time she was able to gain some flexibility and continue to work until the session ended.

Example 2: The minibus was scheduled for each class on a specific day. John knew that Friday morning was his class's time to visit the local community. One week the minibus was unavailable and John was distraught. 'Always Friday, always Friday,' he repeated. Visuals were used to show that the class would go for a local walk to replace the visit, which was accepted as an alternative.

So how can you help the child to understand on those occasions where plans have to change? Firstly, you need to respect and understand the needs of the child while finding ways to reduce the anxiety related to inflexibility.

- Reassure the child that it will be okay.
- Whenever possible, warn of the change in advance – prepare for the change.
- Offer an alternative that will ease the anxiety.

Underlying sensory struggles

'I wish I had known about sensory issues years ago! This information has opened up a whole new understanding for me.'

It's wonderful that we now recognise the impact that sensory issues have on the lives of many of our pupils with autism. By considering these differences, we are more able to support and intervene.

An occupational therapist can provide a professional assessment if sensory issues are suspected. If this is not possible, sensory checklists and assessments are available for your school to use. Does the issue manifest itself in anxiety, behaviour, discomfort or distraction? Once identified, consider what can be done to reduce the impact on the child. Typically, we have focused on the five senses that are familiar to us, but our understanding has to expand to seven:

1 sight
2 hearing
3 smell
4 taste
5 touch
6 proprioception – position and movement
7 vestibular – balance.

Don't underestimate the impact of sensory processing upon learning and behaviour. The presenting issues may be related to hyper-sensitivity or hypo-sensitivity. With 'hyper', sounds may appear louder, smells stronger, touch painful, etc. The child may be experiencing acute awareness when everyone else is oblivious to the same environment. In 'hypo', the child may be under-sensitive to sounds, odours, touch, temperature, etc. Build in time to observe, take a step back and analyse the environment. What is going on at the time? What does the child's body language tell you?

Teaching tip

Record your observations and monitor when similar situations arise to help reinforce (or refute) your assumptions.

Taking it further

Look at Part 10 in detail to develop a clearer understanding of sensory issues, and hold this information at the back of your mind when concerns arise that you cannot easily explain.

A profile shared

'I hadn't realised how many other people had bits of information about David. Until we shared our perspectives and gathered the information into a cohesive profile, we were all letting him down.'

If a range of professionals assess and gather information but the liaison to bring it together does not occur, we miss the opportunity to provide a thorough picture and select the right tools necessary to support. Education, health and care plans (EHCPs) should meet this need to a certain degree but can be unwieldy and inaccessible. This idea helps you to gather all of the information in one easy-to-use profile.

Teaching tip

Although it takes time to distil all of the information into a manageable profile, it is well worth the effort to ensure that the child's needs are expressed in one succinct document that references others as appropriate, e.g. behaviour management plan.

Each service that is involved with a child such as David has valuable information that contributes to the full picture of their needs, strengths and difficulties. No one agency has the monopoly on understanding. Juggling such an abundance of paperwork is time-consuming.

Developing a profile streamlines the information and makes it relevant and accessible. It goes without saying that parents/carers have a vital role to play in both providing information and being aware of the contributions of the many professionals involved in supporting their child. Some contributors are obvious but don't lose sight of the information available from respite providers, siblings, peers and leaders of activities in which the child is involved. One person may hold a key to providing calm or stimulating communication that needs to be shared with the wider support network surrounding the child.

David's profile	
Likes – special interests and favoured activities, peers, spaces, foods, free time	**Dislikes** – transitions, being surprised, group activities, sports...
Communication	**Sensory processing concerns** – sensitive to touch, volume, specific odours, crossing a threshold...
• Receptive – what level of language does David understand when he is spoken to?	
• Expressive – how does David express himself? If verbal, at what level?	**Dietary needs** – special diet, such as gluten or dairy free, additives, limited diet requiring intervention to expand
Medical needs – medication, vision, hearing, physical issues, sleep patterns, toileting needs...	**Behaviour management** – triggers to difficult behaviour; is a behaviour intervention plan required? Guidelines for staff
Strengths – curriculum, physical prowess, factual information, music...	**Attainment** – progress against targets, curriculum, social, communication, managing behaviour, building tolerance
Significant people – family, carers, respite providers, staff in school, professionals	

Providing this succinct profile enables staff to maintain focus on the key issues; the information links to the child's targets across all areas and provides part of the ongoing picture of the child as it is reviewed and updated. Getting this right will reap benefits for all concerned and will underpin the emotional wellbeing of the child.

Taking it further

Where possible, ensure that the pupil contributes to and is aware of the profile – it is not a secret document that talks about the child as if he or she is an outside beneficiary rather than at the heart of understanding.

Overlapping issues

'Until I caught on to the links between Andrew's diverse areas of need, I was compartmentalising my support and targets. When I finally realised how they overlapped and intertwined, I was able to plan appropriately.'

Although the four areas of communication, flexibility, social understanding and sensory issues are described individually in this book, they overlap and must be seen in their relation to each other. Just think about it!

Taking it further

Use a 'teaching moment' to draw attention to difficulties when they arise – for example, 'Your friends walked away because you weren't giving them a chance to enter into the discussion. Remember to take turns when you are speaking in a group. Let's try again.'

Consider these statements expressed by children:

'When sensory issues overwhelm me, I shut down and it's so hard to communicate.'

The shutting down is triggered by the sensory difficulties that the child is experiencing. It may be distraction through sight or sound, but it impedes communication and is seen purely in these terms.

'When things change, my routine is disrupted. I just can't cope. I can't explain why and I just want to be left alone. I don't mean to be aggressive.'

Lack of flexibility with change is at the root of the problem but it is expressed as a behaviour issue. Finding the cause of the behaviour links back to flexibility.

'I find it hard to socialise and then I get too anxious to communicate with the people around me.'

Social isolation and fear of not fitting into the group creates anxiety that impedes communication.

'When I talk about my favourite topic, I know others get bored but I can't stop myself and then the other kids don't want to be with me. It's so frustrating!'

The child is focused on an area of special interest – single-minded interest. This drives peers away and reduces opportunities for socialisation.

How you can help

Socialising cannot happen in isolation, and yet we often focus on one-to-one support and limit social experiences for children with autism. It is not uncommon for an autistic pupil in a mainstream setting to be supported outside of the classroom and not be expected or allowed to participate in the larger group. One example is a child whose parents were asked for her to arrive after the group settled in the room, go home for her dinner and stay inside with a teaching assistant during breaks. This eliminated socialisation throughout the day rather than facilitating social opportunities through phased and planned intervention.

Communication permeates everything we do, through speech, facial expression, body language and gesture, but do we make it a part of groups and relationships in a purposeful way? Do we recognise that inflexibility may have roots in sensory processing and that sensory issues may inhibit social interaction and communication? If we misunderstand the context, we will also misunderstand the support that is needed.

Support interactions through addressing communication and social relationships together; encourage the child to explain why they can only use one particular pencil (for example) and work out the sensory or flexibility issues. By encouraging incidental learning and emphasising the 'why' of difficult situations, you will be consistently supporting the child.

Further examples of how issues overlap are provided in the online resources.

> **Bonus idea** ★
>
> Do your best to analyse situations from the child's perspective, bearing in mind the areas of communication, flexibility, socialisation, and sensory processing. When you are able to recognise the overlapping strands and the impact they have on each other, you will be able to better support the pupil and help them develop coping strategies.

Think visually

'If only I'd realised that every child in my class would benefit from introducing visual systems, I would have started years ago!'

We accept that pupils on the autism spectrum are, for the most part, visual learners. When we present things in words alone, they disappear as soon as they are spoken. Using objects, photographs, symbols and the printed word, alongside spoken language, is more concrete and lasting because the message remains when the words are gone.

Teaching tip

Purposefully make your classroom a visual domain – introduce symbols for quiet, listening, looking and hand-up, and then tap them when they are not followed, reducing the need to repeat reminders verbally.

I confess, I am a visual learner! I follow road signs, I watch for symbols that show me the route to a hospital or a train station, I look at the male/female signage on public toilets, I navigate airports by following the signs and arrows to get to the right gate and into the assigned seat. In fact, I check and double-check my boarding pass to reassure myself of the time and seat. If the information was given to me verbally, I would write it down to look at – to double-check. I understand why children with autism benefit from visual supports.

- Always assume that visuals will be supportive. You may say, 'After assembly, you need your art folder and felt tips', but find that following assembly, there is confusion and you have to start again. If the images or words are on the timetable or whiteboard, they are easily referenced and followed.
- Presenting visual information supports independence – the child does not have to ask you to repeat the words that are forgotten but can see what is happening and what is expected and can get on with it.
- When you feel like a broken record and get exasperated because you have to repeat yourself, remember that using visual reinforcement reduces this and makes it easier for YOU!

Communication essentials

Part 2

Assessment matters

'I was dropped in at the deep end. Adrian was admitted to my class and all I was told was that he was on the autism spectrum. Where do I turn?'

Every school is faced with assessment and sometimes the very word creates a sense of panic! Without being able to understand the child's mode of communication and the level of functioning, it is impossible to provide appropriate intervention and support.

Teaching tip

Refer to the further ideas in Part 2 to support communication and monitor how pupils respond to the strategies. You may be surprised by how changes in *your* communication will positively impact on them!

Method 1

Baseline assessment provides relevant information on the child's level of development when first admitted to the school or provision. Only by having this information can appropriate strategies be defined, individualised targets be outlined and progress be monitored.

As early as possible, glean information from all those who know the pupil best. Parents' insight and perception is essential in recognising how communication has developed and what the current picture is. Professionals involved in assessment, diagnosis and teaching, care providers and others will all have a perspective to offer.

Method 2

If available, analyse assessments that have already been undertaken for Adrian. Clarify the receptive level (what he understands and how this is conveyed) and the expressive level (how he expresses communication). Recognise that these two levels are often very different. The pupil may appear to talk freely (expressive) but if YOU speak TO them in the same way, they may not be able to follow (receptive).

Method 3

If no previous assessments have been undertaken, refer the pupil for a speech and language therapy assessment to determine the current communication issues. Many schools find this difficult due to long waiting lists. If there is an advisory teacher service available, draw on their support for observations and suggestions for appropriate interventions.

Method 4

Observe, carefully watch for communication intent and enable pupils to experience success. If leading you by the hand, discern the reason. If looking confused, offer possible choices either verbally or through objects, photos or symbols.

A list of relevant assessment tools is provided in the online resources.

Bonus idea ★

Rather than asking the child to name common objects, toys and activities, create an exciting game using a selection of items and (with suspense) ask, 'Can you find the cup?', 'Can you find the toothbrush?', etc. Allow time for the child to process the question and locate the object. Follow correct responses with appropriate praise and celebration.

Get my attention!

'My name is not "everyone" or "someone" or "listen up". When you forget to get *my* attention, I don't know you're speaking to me and I get lost in your words.'

Not recognising the subtleties of communication difficulties often faced by children with autism can cause frustration for you and result in confusion for the child. We make many assumptions about understanding, based on the 'norm'. When that expected 'norm' is not internalised by a child, we need to ensure that *our* communication is adapted.

Teaching tip

Ask the children to suggest ways for the group to hear and respond quickly. They may surprise you with their ideas, and their ownership of the method will make them more involved and responsive.

Taking it further

Be creative about getting the child's attention by using an alert sound like a tinkling bell or a clap of your hands. If you explain this, they will catch on and respond, and it will probably help everyone in the group to stop, look and listen.

Our pattern is to think everyone is ready to listen when we want their attention. We use one command to draw the group in and sometimes become just a bit annoyed if all eyes do not turn to the sound of our voice. Difficulty tuning in to group instructions when they are addressed to the entire class rather than to the individual child will often mean children on the spectrum will miss your communication – how will you get their attention?

- Use the child's name – clearly!
- Explain what the cumulative terms mean. Explain that when you say 'everyone', that means *me too*. Emphasise the word and help the child to begin to respond to it. Explain that when you say 'someone', that can be anyone in the group – even that child. If you are asking for someone to run an errand, help the child to realise that they can volunteer, respond and be included. Explain that 'listen up' means pay attention and that you are speaking to the entire group, *including the child*. By teaching these things that the child has not learned incidentally, you will be helping them to improve their understanding and be a better communicator.

What can I use?

'I know some things about autism. I realise that communication is an issue but I'm not sure what is best for Adam and Lilly in my class.'

There is a wealth of material available to support understanding and communication. Finding the *right* interventions for a specific child can be confusing. Referring back to Idea 11, assessment of need is the starting point to discern the way forward.

1 Identifying the child's communication level will form the basis of the system to use. A pre-verbal child may require objects of reference, providing a concrete approach to choice, schedules, etc. This may be followed by photographs alongside the object to move to 2D understanding – and then from photo to symbol to generalise the image. Words added to the symbol lead to recognition and literacy. Eventually, the child may replace symbols with the written word.

2 Building on the above, use verbal commentary to accompany the object, photo, symbol or word to emphasise the verbal label for that specific image. In this way, the language is reinforced and, through repetition, it is hoped that the words will begin to be understood.

3 There are many commercially produced systems and interventions to support communication for children across the autism spectrum. Their appropriateness for the individual must be matched with the assessment of need. PECS (Picture Exchange Communication System®), SCERTS (Social Communication, Emotional Regulation, Transitional Support), Social Stories™ and Comic Strip Conversations are worth considering.

Examples demonstrating pupils' response to strategies are provided in the online resources.

Teaching tip

Part 4 on visual support, structure and routine will help to clarify this further and outline various strategies you can employ.

Taking it further

Access training for the interventions mentioned in point three. Become informed and cascade your learning to your colleagues to further benefit children in your school.

What are you inferring?

'Sometimes the teacher says things that don't make sense to me. Even if I answer him, he acts as if I got it wrong. I never know what to do.'

Without realising it, we assume that our language is clear. This is not an issue for most people receiving our language, and if they are uncertain they will usually ask for clarification. Inference occurs when we make a statement that expects the listener to have the experience to understand our intent. For example, we ask if the child knows where the office is as we hold out the register. The literal answer is 'yes' but the intent of the speaker is for the child to take the register to the office.

Teaching tip

Check yourself. When the child does not seem to understand, or responds in a way that could be interpreted as insolent or cheeky, think back to whether the child got it wrong – or was it you? Pause for thought!

Taking it further

If this is an area of difficulty where you feel a child is not following your direction and appears to be defiant, ask a colleague to observe your interactions. Be open to the voice of a critical friend to improve your practice.

- Ensure that the message sent is the message received! In the above example, the first question should have been followed with, 'Please take the register there.' Be specific; check for understanding to ensure the child can be successful in what you are asking.
- Question or direction? By *asking* if the child would like to sit down or take out his books or put the scraps in the bin, you must be prepared for the answer 'No!' or 'No thank you'. But you are not really asking. You are being polite, when what you really want to say is not 'Would you like to' but 'Please take out your books, sit down, put the scraps in the bin'. When communication is complicated by literal understanding, it becomes a very confusing and frustrating hurdle.
- Use pictures of events or people to help the child infer information from what he or she sees. For example, showing a picture of a sad-looking girl and a broken scooter, ask, 'Why is the girl upset? Would you be upset? What can she do now?'.

Time to think

'When I first heard about "processing time" at a training session, I felt so guilty. I hadn't realised how I was making it impossible for Niklas to respond to my questions.'

Most of us speak quickly and assume everyone can follow. When we listen without distraction, we follow words delivered at speed and take it all in. If you are listening to someone with a different accent, you often find that you need the language to be slowed down and you find yourself concentrating on every word. That is similar to the needs of many children on the autism spectrum.

You may have heard of the 'six-second rule'; the purpose of this is to pause after you speak or ask a question, to let the words sink in. In other words, just slow down! Make a conscious effort to reduce the pace of your delivery, pause and allow thinking and processing time. We often fall into the trap of speaking quickly and then repeating what we have said with the same speed, but twice is not better than once. It isn't easy; it takes resolve and practice.

Teaching tip

Remember Idea 12 – get the child's attention before you begin to speak!

Taking it further

Reinforce your words with appropriate visuals and prompts. For example, hold up the book and the pencil and highlight the activity on the timetable.

Use clear language and, if appropriate, focus on key words. Giving the child time to process enables their response and inclusion in learning. Consider the direction, 'Bring your books and your pencil to the group table, take a seat and wait for me to come.' (Consider it being said quickly!) Try this instead, while standing at the table ready for the group: 'Bring your book and your pencil [pause]; come to the table [while gesturing].' Getting it right first time reduces wasted time and maintains a positive ethos.

Constantly consistent

'I have lots of information about the child but I'm concerned that things are not consistently known and applied across school. I want my team to have shared understanding, terminology and expectations. How can we do this?'

One of the keys to supporting a child with autism is to provide consistency. This is a big ask when we consider the different people, environments, expectations and resources that the child encounters every day.

Teaching tip

When something unexpected occurs, ask the question 'Why?' and take the time for all contributors to unravel the problem.

Bonus idea ★

The title of any profile is important! Is it child-centred or written *about* the child, e.g. 'Things I want you to know about me' or 'Alix Brown's profile'? Consider the difference in the way the information is approached. If we can hear the child's voice, we are both asking for their contribution in any way we can and attempting to analyse *from the child's point of view*. If we are thinking it through from our adult perspective, can we be sure it reflects the individual?

Remember:

- Sharing information about the child is crucial. Unless there is a shared understanding of the way in which the child communicates, responds to others, copes within the environment and processes sensory information, as well as likes and dislikes, it is impossible to create the consistency you're striving for.
- Create a pupil profile as outlined earlier in this topic. Be concise and ensure that it is a 'living' document – regularly reviewed and revised to keep abreast of change and progress.
- Consider how to make the information available for reference while maintaining confidentiality. The importance of confidentiality balanced with accessibility is discussed in the online resources.
  - A classroom file may be useful but not if it stays unopened on a shelf.
  - Information on the classroom noticeboard can work but consider whether it will be seen by those without authority.
  - A clipboard with a cover sheet could be readily accessible by staff, easy to revise and available for classroom briefings.

The age of technology

'I realise how lucky we are to be surrounded by technology. It really does help make my job easier.'

This is another area where assessment is essential. One size does not fit all. Exploring the range of technology available for use is the first step. What are the needs and how are they best met?

Low-to-medium technology includes:
- BIGmack – a single-message speech-generating device
- talking photo album
- voice amplifier – encouraging vocalisation
- audio books.

These devices provide simple forms of helping a child to be interested in communication, or make a simple request or comment. For example, the BIGmack can be activated to request the toilet independently. A pair of buttons can be used to indicate like and dislike of activities, enabling the child to have a voice.

High technology includes:
- computers
- electronic tablets
- Proloquo2go – symbol-based communication app
- portable word processors
- text to speech and speech to text
- Augmentative Alternative Communication (AAC) devices
- interactive whiteboard.

Some staff may be familiar with many of these devices, but in order for them to benefit the child's communication, they must be fit for purpose and the upkeep and maintenance must be a priority. Consistency is essential and an uncharged battery can create high anxiety.

Further information and examples of the use of communication or technology aids are available in the online resources.

Teaching tip

The use of the interactive whiteboard can bring communication and learning to life. It provides a wonderful interactive way to begin the day, enables stimulating and motivating curriculum presentation, and enables children to explore, play and learn!

Taking it further

Support a member of staff to access training in assistive technology. Developing expertise within the school will make it possible for the school to keep up to date, be abreast of new developments and understand the maintenance of products used by children.

An entrance to music

'A colleague told me about using music to support communication. I'd really like to know more.'

Using music to enable and enhance communication has long been an approach used with Early Years and primary-aged children in both mainstream and special schools. We all recognise how a tune can be 'stuck in our head' and this can be a powerful tool for learning and responding. Music can be used to set the mood, provide a bridge from one activity to the next, or create group and turn-taking opportunities. Through music, children can learn to relax and to be active.

Transitions throughout the day can be difficult for children with autism, from arriving at school in the morning to moving between activities and changing physical locations. Beginnings and endings should be clear and prepare the child for what comes next. Using music to signal these changes can create a smooth transition. Coming into the classroom at the start of the day with a familiar tune can be part of your welcome. Be consistent about the chosen piece so that it becomes associated with the specific activity. Music as a support for the visual timetable can become part of the predictability and reassurance of the day. Consider a lively tune for tidy-up time – when the music begins, it gives a signal that resources need to be put away and that the children participate in this. Time to go for lunch? In one school, I heard 'Food, Glorious Food' begin to play as the children prepared to line up to go to the dining room.

Using age-appropriate songs can enhance curriculum learning by supporting the various topics undertaken in primary school classrooms. Singing about the planets with visuals on the interactive whiteboard is much more enticing than a verbal presentation – particularly for children who have a strength in visual learning!

Teaching tip

Be creative – make up your own songs for greetings, gaining attention and reinforcing learning. Could the children help with this?

Taking it further

Both Sing Up and the BBC have some excellent songs you could use at the following links: https://www.singup. org/singup-songbank/ top-ten-playlists/top-ten-curriculum-songs/ http://www.bbc.co.uk/ schoolradio/subjects/ music

Bonus idea ★

By sharing enjoyable responses to music with the home, this strategy can improve relaxation and positive together-time for the family.

Don't take it literally

'Sometimes the teacher says something that leaves me very confused and then he is annoyed with me if I didn't get it right.'

Our language is not always as clear as we consider it to be. We use different terms to mean the same thing. For example, we say 'Listen up' but we also say 'Quiet down'. What does it actually mean to listen up? Idioms create confusion if you take them literally.

- Be aware of the language you use. Seek clarity and be alert to when the child shows confusion or misunderstanding. If you ask a question rather than giving an instruction, be prepared for an honest answer and do not misinterpret it as disrespectful. Give a polite direction rather than an option.
- When something is misunderstood, *explain the meaning* so that it is understood when encountered the next time. Common idioms like 'it cost an arm and a leg' are confusing and leave visual images that lead to misunderstanding. Examples of literal misunderstandings, to raise awareness of this issue, are provided in the online resources.
- You may sometimes consider that the child is rude in the way in which they speak to you. For example, if the child corrects you when you have made a factual error, it is just something that comes naturally and the child thinks you would appreciate this knowledge being shared with you. If the child points out that you have a spot on your face, it is just a fact and not meant to be rude. Don't take it personally! Recognise this as part of the different way of perceiving the world, and gently point out inappropriate comments and help the child understand that some things are better not mentioned at all or mentioned personally rather than in public.

Taking it further

Try reading this great book: *It's Raining Cats and Dogs: An Autism Spectrum Guide to the Confusing World of Idioms, Metaphors and Everyday Expressions.*

Bonus idea ★

Plan a fun lesson using idioms. Illustrate the literal meaning of each idiom using a visual and ask pupils to search for the idiomatic meaning.

It's more than words

'Words, words, words. My teacher doesn't seem to understand that she talks too much and does things with her voice and face that I just don't understand.'

We need to recognise how we are communicating with children, and how we can augment that communication and ensure that *our dependence* on the spoken word is not dominating the way we receive and deliver messages to the children.

Teaching tip

Record positive communication that you observe during the day – build on the early foundations and consider how you can foster next steps. Jotting down on sticky notes is quick, and if you are really well organised, you can colour code them for different areas of progress.

Taking it further

Facilitate conversations on a shared topic and support the progress that can be made. Be aware that these skills need to be generalised across settings, so keep an eye out for casual conversations throughout the day.

Method 1

Use your skills of observation to discover how the child is trying to communicate with you. Does the pre-verbal child glance at a desired object, indicating that it is wanted? Hold the object and name it, matching it to a photograph or symbol if this method is being used. Does the child take you by the hand and lead you to the sink, for example? Is this indicative of thirst? Gesture 'drink?' and then offer the drink, reinforcing the word.

Method 2

Some of the children you are supporting may be using limited language. Expand the vocabulary with key words, e.g. if the child says 'toilet', respond with 'I want the toilet'. A word of caution – it is the child who wants the toilet and you are modelling their language in this sentence. If you say that 'you want the toilet', the child may develop pronoun confusion when beginning to use simple sentences and refer to self as you.

Method 3

You may work with children who have very strong verbal skills but fail to engage in dialogue appropriately. Teach the skills of turn-taking, listening to the other speaker(s), personal space, body language and gesture. By ignoring dominance of the conversation, the child may be socially excluded.

Getting the environment right

Part 3

Environmental audit

'As a mainstream teacher, I focused on providing a stimulating environment, and discovering the need to tone it down was a real challenge for me.'

Primary schools are well known for creating an environment that reflects 'all things bright and beautiful'. For your pupils with autism, the colourful birds and the buzzing bees may make listening and learning an overwhelming challenge. Looking at the environment through the eyes of your pupils is not easy, but once you put on the autism-tinted lenses, you'll be amazed at what you see!

Teaching tip

You will find the characteristics listed in table format to offer a tick list for your self-audit in the online resources.

Put aside your assumptions and take an objective look at your classroom and reflect on your findings. Your audit should consider:

- Lighting – any buzzing sounds?
- Natural light – blinds on the windows to reduce glare?
- Flooring – used to signify discrete areas?
- Clearly defined areas for specific purposes?
- Flooring – to cushion sound?
- Colours – low stimulation?
- Patterns – too busy?
- Mobiles – obscuring space?
- Display – purposeful and well maintained?
- Access to quiet area?
- Access to playground?
- Position of work area – reduced distraction?
- Organisation – clear labels on drawers and cupboards?
- Organisation – resources available for child to access?
- Corridors – clear and easy to navigate?
- Dining area – are acoustics abrasive?
- Health and safety – storage of hazardous materials.
- Health and safety – assessment of resources that may cause risk.
- Health and safety – management of climbers and runners.

Invite a critical friend to assess your audit and reflect on the space with you. Be open to suggestions and consider ways to improve the environment to make it user-friendly. Create a balance between stimulating and purposeful display and the need for reduced distraction.

When you are satisfied that you know where you need to make adjustments to the environment, be brave and creative in establishing the changes. Look at the consistency across the school in relation to the needs of individual children and groups. Balance the needs of the children with autism with those of the peer group, but do ensure that reasonable adjustments are not denied.

Taking it further

Check out *The Autism Inclusion Toolkit* by Lynn Plimley and Maggie Bowen. This will provide you with a wealth of information to support you in ensuring that your school is developing effective strategies to support pupils on the autism spectrum.

Are you sitting comfortably?

'Why doesn't he sit still and focus like the other children in the class?'

Many factors within the environment influence the child's ability to focus and learn. Following an audit to identify concerns, what can you implement to provide the RIGHT environment?

Of course, environment is not limited to the physical organisation and structure you provide. Creating an ordered, structured space that exudes calm is essential.

- Sitting on the floor can be uncomfortable for some, while others see it as a place to move about. Try a small mat or a cushion. It designates the spot as well as softening the floor. You may relate it to the child's special interest, e.g. superheroes.
- Classroom chairs are not always comfortable. Ball chairs and 'wobble' cushions are a great alternative that can make a real difference to children with proprioceptive issues, such as the need to move to ensure that they are stable.
- For some children, being too near to peers can create discomfort and distraction. Try seating the child at the front of the group, where the teacher is the focus and can gently, quietly reassure – or at the back of the group, where there is no interference from behind. Take time to explain personal space and accidental touch to all children. Make it fun!
- So many children struggle to stand in a queue. Once again, this can be a matter of personal space and an aversion to touching others; some children may misinterpret the casual brushing against that is inevitable with children. Spacing is the key. Try to place the child with autism first in the queue or last in the queue. Teach children to stay an arm's length away from others when queuing up. Footprints painted on the floor to designate where to stand can be helpful.

Clear the clutter!

'I do try to keep the classroom tidy but clutter does get on top of me sometimes. Does it really matter?'

Life in a classroom is busy and there are many demands on you as a teacher, from the time you arrive in the morning until the time you leave late in the afternoon. Priorities of planning and record-keeping, meetings and extracurricular commitments eat away at time for tidying up but keeping a tidy environment really does matter.

Lack of organisation that results from clutter can be frustrating for you and for many of your children. It leads to things being mislaid, inaccessible and often less than well maintained. There are some simple ways to tackle the problem:

- Keep your eyes open to the appearance of your room, surfaces, noticeboards, desk, etc. At times, we are so used to what we see that we fail to recognise that things have gotten out of hand.
- Use the children to help you. You are not doing any favours to your pupils or their parents/carers if you are tidying up after them! You may develop a jobs rota or you may have a set routine of clearing up, organising and tidying at the end of sessions.
- You may have classroom monitors with an area of the room to take pride in. Help the children to see responsibility as a reward, enticing everyone to get involved.

Teaching tip

Remember that some of the things you make with the children are important because of the *process*, not because of the *product*, and may not need to be kept in the longer term.

Bonus idea ★

Have a 'catch all' container for things that do not have an appointed place in the room and set aside a time at the end of the week to clear it. Some of it may fit best in the bin – don't be afraid to get rid of extraneous clutter that does not serve a purpose.

Reasonable adjustments

'Sometimes it seems unfair to the rest of the class to change things just for Jay.'

The Equality Act (2010) refers to the need to make *reasonable adjustments* to accommodate for individuals with a disability. Autism is a recognised disability and falls under this advice.

We would never dream of denying a hearing-impaired pupil a hearing aid or a visually impaired pupil a pair of glasses. We would never consider asking a child with a mobility issue to participate in the same PE activities as an able-bodied pupil. But I have often had staff express concern that changing the environment – providing a specialist chair or a work station, for example – is 'not fair to the other children'. Really? Consider the needs of the individual pupil by reviewing their personal profile and assessments. Remember that the child may have additional needs such as dyspraxia and sensory issues that require adjustments.

Raise awareness by developing a child-friendly presentation to explain what autism is and to help the peer group to understand the need for specialist resources and differentiated support and management. Use examples such as children wearing glasses and other individual needs, e.g. a plaster cast after a broken arm, a pencil grip or writing slope, a higher or lower chair. Help the children to understand that autism is a 'hidden disability', and not easily recognised.

Some modifications may be appropriate for the entire class. For example, if a visual timetable is used for the child with autism, prepare a whole-class timetable to present the routine of the day visually. There isn't a child in your group who would not benefit from this!

The quiet corner

'Sometimes I can tell she is getting anxious and just needs a place to chill but how can I provide that in a busy classroom? There just isn't enough space for everything.'

There are times within the day when breaks are absolutely essential for reducing stress and enabling calm. Developing an area in the classroom for this is both possible and necessary.

Do you ever feel like curling up in a corner and relaxing when the pressure gets to be too much? We all do! When pupils are responding to the high expectations of being in a group and participating in activities, as well as applying themselves to the curriculum, it can all become too much. Add to this the sensory issues that can at times be overwhelming, and a quiet area begins to make abundant sense. Providing a comfortable bolt hole to relax in, away from the hustle and bustle of the group, can make the difference between coping and unravelling.

Analyse the space. Look for a low-traffic area away from doors and the glare of windows. Drape some fabric to enclose the space and add soft, comfortable cushions and a blanket or throw to curl up in. Soft toys and stress-reducing resources, such as squeeze balls and stretchy toys support calming. Could you play some quiet music or add fairy lights? Be creative without going over the top.

Remember, this is not a sensory room; it's a quiet corner, an accessible retreat from the busy classroom for taking a much-needed break.

Teaching tip

A quiet corner does not need to break the budget. Try looking for fabric in a charity shop or fabric shop bargain corner. Send a message out to staff and parents/carers for fabrics, textures and cushions. You may even have a parent volunteer who could do some creative sewing.

Taking it further

Make it a classroom project, with the children designing and helping to add comforts like beanbags and soft toys.

But where do I work?

'I wish I knew how to get Wei to focus but he watches everyone else and I have to constantly remind him to get on with his own activities. I get so frustrated!'

The hustle and bustle of a classroom diverts attention from learning — planning the workspace to suit the individual needs of a child is a must. It will not only benefit the pupil and their independence but will also remove your need to be a 'nag'!

Teaching tip

Do remember that this is a 'reasonable' adjustment. The online resources for this book further discuss the importance of an appropriate work area.

Sitting in a group with the inevitable fidgeting and interruptions of peers is often too distracting for a child with autism. Try carving out a work area by placing a desk or table in a position that faces the wall on the perimeter of the classroom. Label it as a 'work station' and if the child is using a visual timetable, have it available in the space for easy reference. Reduce distraction as much as possible by, for example, ensuring the desk is not in front of a window or surrounded by displays.

Do include the child in a group setting for appropriate times of the day, to encourage peer relationships and participation in activities, and gradually work towards greater time and independence in this setting. By having a clearly defined, low-distraction work area, you are giving the child a greater chance of success in focusing on and completing tasks.

If you are worried about the child being isolated by this, try having a double work station with a peer who could be a good role model, and have them work side by side. You may even consider more than one peer on a rotational basis to ensure that the child is developing a closer physical presence with a range of other children in the group.

What does low arousal mean?

'I can't stimulate the rest of the group if I have to cut down on displays for one or two children. It isn't right.'

'Low arousal' refers to approaches in the environment that aid concentration through providing calm and order. Limit distractions by considering volume, acoustics, colour, lighting, clear organisation and purposeful display.

You do not need or want a clinical, sterile-looking classroom or school, but it is sometimes noticeable that school corridors and classroom walls look as if it was impossible to discern what to display, so everything has been added over time and takes up almost every square inch of the wall space. It can be overwhelming and even painful to a child with visual sensory overload issues.

Consider some of these options:

- A display board outside the classroom for current topic work.
- Designated spaces in the classroom for curriculum focus but not covering entire walls.
- 3D cubes or pyramids on group tables with prompts and information, rather than multiple mobiles dangling from the ceiling.
- Use of photographs celebrating children's accomplishments and bringing the activities back to life for reflection and recall – try to include all children.
- Clear surfaces to create a clean and well-organised appearance.
- Well-organised and clearly labelled resources in suitable storage units.
- Scaled-down displays in the corridors and shared spaces to maintain a well-ordered and planned environment.

This environmental issue is further explored in the online resources.

> **Bonus idea**
>
> Instead of displaying all work on boards, let the children develop scrap books of their stories, artwork, diagrams, etc. Have them in the reading corner to be enjoyed and shared. Use them on parents' evenings for parents to peruse while they wait for their appointment. Photograph albums showing participation and achievement can affirm and bring enjoyment to memories of past events.

Busy places – HELP!

'He seems to be okay in the classroom but when we go to assembly or dinner it's like he's a different child.'

The environment is not limited to the pupil's individual classroom. Reducing stress and enabling coping in the class base is great, but unless the entire school recognises the pupil's needs, the day will remain stressful and fraught.

Be consciously aware of when and where the pupil begins to show signs of anxiety and inability to cope. Common situations are:
- entering and exiting the school
- corridors
- cloak rooms
- dining room
- assembly
- playground.

In each of these settings, the children are in close proximity to each other and noise levels have generally risen. There is less structure and the sense of 'order' and predictability is diminished. For most of your children, this is a gift – free at last! It's a time for chatting, socialising and playing. These very things are anxiety-raising for children with autism.

Be alert to signs of heightened anxiety. Try to identify specific issues and address them.

- If the volume in a room is too high, ensure that ear defenders are available.
- If there is too much commotion in the corridor, allow the child to exit slightly before or enter slightly after peers.
- If the child is at a loss in the playground, organise an appropriate peer to act as a 'playground buddy', and ensure staff are alert to issues.
- Is the dining room acoustically friendly? Clattering dishes can be excruciating for a child with sensitive hearing! Try to provide an appropriate space for a small group to eat away from this environment.

Defeated by distractions

'I've worked really hard on reducing the visuals in my classroom but at times Suri still gets distressed and I just don't know why.'

There are so many different and competing interferences in our environment that it's sometimes difficult to recognise them. This is where your powers of observation come in. It is so helpful to have time to look and listen attentively to solve the mystery.

Here are some examples of situations where distractions cause distress.

Sally and James
One of the other children in the class periodically makes a shrill sound. Most of the children ignore it but Sally is so distracted that she can no longer engage. No easy answers – James will continue to make the noise as part of his communication. Reassure Sally: 'It's only James. It's okay.' Be consistent about this and then turn it around. 'Sally, what was that noise?' You are looking for her to say, 'Only James.' Inject some humour into the exchange to relax Sally and give her the confidence to ignore the sound.

Dawud
Dawud seems to be getting on with his activity well when he suddenly shrieks and takes cover under the table. No one else is aware of any change in the environment. It happens periodically and each time there is confusion about why. Aha! Dawud has a fear of dogs. The school is in a residential area and there are times when a local dog uses its voice. Dawud cannot discern the distance the dog is from school – that he is safe, that there is no danger. Knowing the problem can then lead to staff working together to help Dawud understand that the dog is not a danger to him – he is safe. The online resources further explore the wide range of distractions that may create barriers to learning and provide supportive ideas.

Teaching tip

A Social Story™ may be an appropriate way to support a pupil like Dawud. Share the concern and solutions with his parents/carers to ensure a consistent approach. Check out *The New Social Story Book* by Carol Gray. The NAS website has information about Social Stories™ that you may find useful: http://www.autism.org. uk/about/strategies/ social-stories-comic- strips.aspx.

Bonus idea

Many schools are making use of therapy dogs for a range of reasons. Perhaps your schools could try introducing Dawud to a therapy dog to reduce his fear.

Safe and secure

'I feel like I have to have eyes in the back of my head.'

There is no question that some children test the boundaries and diligence is essential. There may be issues with climbing, running off, ingesting inedibles or appearing to have no fear of danger.

It is important to have a full profile of the pupil, the risks and hazards. It is also important that consideration is given to the 'balance of risk' as we work to support children to take managed risks and not impede their development of independence and decision-making.

External – Most special and specialist schools have a secure, fenced boundary to ensure children are not able to leave the site and put themselves in danger. This is not always the case in mainstream schools and attention must be paid to the risk of a child who may wander off. What precautions has your school put in place?

Internal – Many schools manage doors through electronic fobs to prevent children wandering to areas that are out of bounds, e.g. storage cupboards, staffrooms, food and design technology areas and hazardous substances cupboards. A swimming pool can pose clear danger without consistent caution. Ensure that all areas are risk-assessed and appropriate precautions are put in place.

Classrooms – For a child who ingests inedible objects, it is necessary to ensure that nothing of a toxic nature is accessible. Even resources such as glue, paint and modelling materials need to be monitored. Are sharp implements such as scissors safe in your room or are they a potential risk?

Playground – Are there any vulnerable areas where climbing can pose a risk? Is the equipment in good working order? Are the children trained to use equipment safely, e.g. not to walk behind a swing in motion?

Bonus idea ★

Establish scheduled environmental walks across the entire school site, both internal and external. Take a child's-eye view of your classroom, on your knees, looking at what may be a potential hazard for the child.

Visual support, structure and routine

Part 4

Make it predictable

'When Charlie joined my class I didn't know what hit me. If he didn't know exactly what the day held, he asked me over and over again. It really did get to me!'

Given that change is one of the challenges within autism that leads to anxiety, making the day/week/schedule predictable for Charlie is necessary to help him relax, be confident and cope. But think about it – *you* know what your day holds; you almost certainly use your written or electronic diary and check it regularly, have a daily class timetable to refer to, know what time sessions begin and end, etc. Without all of that, you too would struggle.

Supporting through visuals can begin as soon as the children arrive at your classroom door. Are there any changes today? Is there a visitor? A new child starting? A new member of staff? Have a 'CHANGES TODAY' label on the door to forewarn children and parents or carers.

- Provide an age-appropriate timetable of the day's events. Consider whether the entire day is too much for the age or understanding of your pupils. Perhaps a half or quarter day is best.
- Carefully consider where the visual timetable is positioned so that it is visible to all. Size is important – too small and it cannot be referenced from across the room.
- The timetable is a 'working document' rather than a static display. Refer to it as activities begin and end. If you use individual pieces to denote different activities, remove them as the activity comes to an end, clarifying that X has finished and Y is about to begin.

Troubling transitions

'I always thought of transitions as the start of a new year or new school. Dealing with micro transitions throughout the day is a real challenge.'

Moving from one location, task or activity to another is difficult for many children with autism. Support transition through appropriate strategies to make these times manageable.

Most of your children take the movement of the day in their stride, and when you verbally declare that an activity has finished or you clap your hands to indicate time to stop, they respond. For some children, the abrupt nature of this is just too much and creates anxiety, often leading to a refusal to comply. If you know this and do not alter your way of drawing activities to a close, the resulting behaviours will prevail. Try these strategies:

- Get the children's attention through a recognised sound, e.g. a clap, a tambourine or a bell.
- Give a warning that the activity will end in a set time, e.g. five minutes, two minutes.
- Reinforce the time with a visual, e.g. timer on the interactive whiteboard, sand timer or electronic timer.
- When the time is up, clearly state that the activity is finished.
- If the children need to tidy resources away, make this clear and, if appropriate, play some tidy up music that is suitable in length.
- Refer to the group and/or visual timetable to remove the finished activity and be clear about what is happening next.
- For children who are using 'First... Then' (or 'Now... Next') visuals, provide this information as the new activity begins, to reassure them of what will follow.

The online resources provide further links to tools to support transition.

Teaching tip

By planning ahead and developing a rhythm for transitions throughout the day, you will be reducing anxiety and paving a smooth pathway for success.

Taking it further

Macro transitions from year to year and changes to a new school are hugely important and require a multi-professional approach that is planned well in advance. The provision plan needs to be underpinned with visuals related to the environment, staff, things that change and things that stay the same. Only through thorough preparation will the pupil feel secure and move on successfully.

They're *my* targets

'We were setting targets for the children but began to realise that they were really for the adults. How do we express them in child-friendly terms and truly engage the pupils?'

Too often, targets are set *by* staff and *for* staff without enabling the child to participate, recognise and own the targets. Translating targets into child-friendly form supports ownership.

Taking it further

When the target is achieved, take it a step further to challenge further progress. In this example, that could mean expanding the number of children in the game, helping Jakob to develop skills of participating with more children, or encouraging Jakob to initiate the game, thus increasing independence in play situations.

This is a common problem and really does take away the child's ability to develop a focus on their own goals. For example, you may have set the target 'Jakob to take turns playing a game with a peer'. *You* set up the game, *you* observe and record the outcomes. But why not look at this target through Jakob's eyes? The target becomes: 'To play a game with one of my friends and take turns'.

- Adults should support Jakob's target through a written or photographic list of friends he has nominated and can choose from.
- Provide a list or visual choice board of turn-taking games Jakob likes to play.
- Monitor and facilitate as appropriate.
- Ask Jakob and his friend whether they enjoyed the game and whether they took turns fairly. This may be verbal or may be through the use of well-understood visuals such as ✗ ✓ or ☺ ☹.
- The target has now become Jakob's target, enabling him to take responsibility, giving him choice and developing his relationship with peers who may begin to recognise Jakob's ability to contribute to enjoyable activities.

Practical examples of pupil targets are provided and explained in the online resources.

The *right* timetable

'I have a number of children with autism in my group and made the same timetable for each one of them. It worked for some but others couldn't cope. Where did I go wrong?'

It is common to assume that all of the children on the autism spectrum are the same. When you recognise the individual presentation of autism, you begin to fine-tune the strategies and resources you use.

The first consideration has to be the specific needs and development of the child. What has your assessment (Idea 11) shown regarding the communication and development needs? Is the child pre-verbal and requiring objects of reference, photographs or symbols? For example, a cup might be used to denote 'drink' on a tactile timetable. A photograph of a cup or an icon or drawing of a cup may be used depending on the needs of the child. Is the child literate and requiring the printed word or symbols supported by words? Can the child cope with a whole day, half day or quarter day presentation of the timetable? Does the child need a 'First... Then...' timetable with only two activities presented at one time?

Remember that individual timetables complement the group timetable, which provides information for the whole class.

Individualised timetables to address a range of issues are provided in the online resources.

Teaching tip

The security of the timetable and the predictability it provides supports the pupil to cope with the routine. One frequent mistake is withdrawing the timetable *because* the child is coping, and then wondering why anxiety heightens. Sometimes the reason given is that the timetable is 'too immature'. If this is the case, develop a new age-appropriate timetable to meet changing needs. To remove the timetable outright is equal to taking away a child's glasses because with them they can see!

Warning ahead

'Just when I think we have the visual support right, something happens that throws Joseph into an absolute panic!'

If things go wrong, the important thing to do is to analyse the cause of distresss and to consider how it could have been proactively avoided or planned for. Never be dismissive of the child's reaction to sudden change and disappointment. It's not easy to take things in your stride when you need predictability and routine.

Teaching tip

Do your best to put yourself in the child's shoes. Have you ever been disappointed by a sudden change of plans? How did you react?

Here are some common examples of changes and how you could plan for them:

Supply teacher or teaching assistant to take the class

If known in advance, explain. If not known in advance, explain when the child arrives at school. If necessary, provide a photo of the supply staff.

Planned community visit is postponed

Explain why and use a calendar to show when it will occur – how many days? Assure the child that the visit will happen.

Lunch menu changes due to unforeseen circumstances

Visually show new options and enable the child to choose. Can you offer an alternative if none suffice? Is there a fall-back of fruit and toast available, for example?

Transport is late to pick the child up

Explain this to the child and offer a favoured activity. Don't state a number of minutes; use words like 'soon' and 'in a little while'.

Fire drill

For many reasons, including sensory ones, the fire drill can be a traumatic event for many children. Reassurance and comfort are essential. Use visuals to explain the sequence of the drill and the reason for it. Ensure that a member of staff supports the child. Offer ear defenders if appropriate.

In the playground

'Kieran has adjusted so well to classroom routine but really struggles to engage in anything in the playground. He just stands or wanders aimlessly. What can I do?'

This scenario is common for children on the autism spectrum during unstructured time. When you thrive on routine and following a pattern, deciding what to do in open spaces during free time is a challenge. While most children can't wait to chat with friends and play together, the child with autism is often left feeling vulnerable and alone.

Try supporting children like Kieran through:

- Creating a circle of friends to help engage him in activities he can participate in. Remember that team sports may not be his forte but playing on the climbing frame and copying actions may be. One way to do this is to have a list of classmates who are willing to support, and rota them through the week so that they also have days to do their own thing with friends. Imposing peer support is not always a positive thing for Kieran or the other child.
- Giving him a part to play. If he likes watching the footballers but struggles to be a team player, could he be encouraged to keep score or to return the ball when it goes out of bounds? This gives him a role and connects him to his peers.
- Developing a choice board in the playground to help him select activities and resources. A large board with laminated photos of the available equipment will help to make Kieran and others aware of the options he can choose. Leaving it to him to seek out equipment is unlikely to motivate him.

The online resources elaborate on how to maximise play and learning in the playground.

Teaching tip

Helping Kieran to participate with others and get some exercise at break time is important but you also need to be aware that, after the demands of the classroom, Kieran may need some down time to just tune out, and you should respect the balance between the two.

Bonus idea ★

Have a friendship bench in the playground. Locate it away from the hustle and bustle of active play and encourage peer buddies to share this space with Kieran when he wants to be away from the crowd.

Transparently clear

'Esma doesn't always understand the instructions I've given the group and I wish I knew how to help her follow along more readily.'

Sometimes we expect children to pick up the inferences we make when we give tasks to children. This is another area of difficulty for your children on the autism spectrum.

Taking it further

The TEACCH system offers great benefits to task organisation for pupils with autism. Check it out at https://teacch.com. Practical suggestions to make the most of the TEACCH system are explored in the online resources.

Consider, for example, your instruction for the group to find and list as many African animals as they can. There is no clear ending here; this task can go on forever and ever. I worked with a family whose son would not go to bed because his homework assignment was framed in this way. But what do you mean by setting this task? Are the children to search for as many as they can in half an hour or up to a certain limit? The lack of clarity feeds the anxiety of a child who does not have a cut-off.

For another child, working in a workbook, the instruction was to do the maths questions on page three. The questions were finished before the session ended and he went on to page four and five, without understanding the concepts on those pages, and was incorrect in his work. The solution was to place a red dot at the end of the section where he should stop. Helping him to put the red dot in place when he started his assignment gave him responsibility for following the instruction correctly.

A clear indication of what is expected is necessary. In contrast to the examples above, some children will accomplish very little because they are not sure how much work is expected. For example, if providing a set of basket tasks without a clear visual matching the baskets with 123, ABC or picture matching, the child will not understand how to approach the tasks or when the tasks have been completed.

How long will this last?

'Michael has no concept of time and repeatedly asks me how much longer. It really does become annoying at times.'

If a child has no concept of time, they have no way of knowing when an activity will end, no way of knowing whether they have time to finish what they're doing and no idea how soon it is until they can have a break! I, for one, look at my watch quite a lot and feel distracted when I have forgotten it or if the battery dies.

Prepare the child for change by providing a clear ending to an activity. An abrupt stop often causes frustration leading to anger. For example, if a child is having time on the computer or tablet and is told to stop, the reaction is very likely to be negative. If, however, a five minute warning is given, a further reminder at one minute and a clear, 'time on the tablet is finished', the child is enabled to accept the situation. Similarly, if the child is engaged in a chosen activity such as Lego™ and no warning is given, it is difficult to save the partially made model. With a warning, the precious product can be safely set aside for completion at a later time.

Idea 34 suggests one way to help children understand what comes next. This alone, however, will not give them an indication of the passing of time. Making it concretely visual for them will ease their anxiety and help them to cope. There are a number of resources to support this. They include:

- sand timers in various graduated minutes
- large timer on the interactive whiteboard
- counting-down clocks that show the time left very clearly
- electronic timers
- traffic light symbols, e.g. green for go, amber to warn that the activity is coming to an end, red to show STOP.

Teaching tip

Use your judgement. Do not choose a resource that will become a fixation – your aim is to support the child and clarify time, not to transfix them with a product.

Taking it further

Do remember that keeping track of time is something that every child in your group will benefit from – as will you!

Let me choose

'It's so easy to make choices for the children and to think I know their minds. I am beginning to realise this takes away their right to express opinions.'

All children have the right to choose! We actually impede their development and independence if we do not begin to respect their personal preferences. I can hear you asking the question, 'Does that mean there are no boundaries?'. No, it doesn't, but it does mean providing real, meaningful options.

Teaching tip

Bear in mind that 'variety is not the spice of life' for your children on the autism spectrum. Too many choices can be overwhelming and distracting. Avoid offering the same choices all the time by introducing some new options that will widen experiences and opportunities. Visual examples of individualised choice boards are provided in the online resources.

Choice boards are not just for play and activity time. They can be used to develop choice and communication throughout the day, including:

- choosing preferred equipment needed for a task
- colours for use in diagrams and artwork
- meal choices in the dining room
- equipment at playtime
- sensory resources for breaks
- peer or staff to work with.

I observed a very positive rebound therapy session where choices were provided throughout: choice of how many jumps, choice of peer to share the trampoline with, choice of staff member to bounce with, choice of colour of bean bag for a bouncing game. Real choices were identified through speech or visuals on a choice board. The enjoyment of the session was evident throughout. The relaxation was pervasive. The preferences of the children were respected and valued.

A picture paints a thousand words

'I think I'm very good with words. I describe things to my class and expect them to build on that. My children with autism just don't seem to get it and I have to explain over and over again.'

Many people with autism find imagination very difficult. If you adopt an abstract approach, your ideas will not be accessible to all. You will have to alter *your* style to give the pupils the opportunity to participate and succeed.

Let's say, for example, that you are describing the lifestyle of children in the Victorian era. For most of your group, your descriptive language will create pictures in their minds and they'll get it! They'll laugh appropriately when you talk about some of the games they played – no technology, etc. They'll show concern when you talk about working in the mills and injuries, food and hygiene. But words alone are insufficient for some of your pupils.

Method 1 – Bring the words alive with videos and graphics on the interactive whiteboard. This will put the children in the picture. They will see what life was like and, by pausing to point out detail, you will consolidate meaning.

Method 2 – Use photographs and pieces of art that can be looked at again and again with growing awareness of the detail.

Method 3 – Have a dress-up day to contrast the school uniform with children's attire during the Victorian period. Play the part of the Victorian teacher by dressing as a teacher of the day, and sensitively become the stern master or miss of that time period. (I say 'sensitively' because I played this role in a school, and one child burst into tears when I scolded a classmate for having dirty hands!)

Taking it further

Take learning outside the classroom to visit an appropriate museum or estate. Providing the atmosphere of long ago can reinforce learning in a concrete and atmospheric way.

Social opportunities

Part 5

Good morning!

'As hard as I try, Mark seldom responds to my morning hello and never initiates interaction. I wish I could find a way to solve this.'

Many children with autism are aloof and do not see the need to greet or bid farewell. Providing prompts and giving meaning to this social norm begins to support social relationships.

Teaching tip

Developing this skill is an important part of polite social awareness and a life skill for engaging with society, but never force the issue if the child cannot cope on a specific occasion. Heightening stress will not make this a natural development.

Teaching tip

Echolalia is the involuntary repetition of sounds and words.

One of the first things that struck me when I entered the world of autism education was the lack of response from my new group of children. Being used to chatter, hugs and everyone wanting to share their news at once, I felt deskilled and devalued in some way. The main responders were children with echolalia, who returned my 'Hello, how are you?' just as I said it to them.

We are social; we smile, greet, nod and share news, and expect others to do the same. When children look past us and ignore our approaches, we don't always understand, often just ignoring the rebuff. Here are some ideas to help you out.

1   Greeting someone or saying goodbye are social skills that have not been learnt through osmosis and need to be directly taught. Try puppets to get the point across, using them to ignore each other and then get it right, by facing each other, acknowledging and greeting or saying goodbye.

2   Have the children make posters to be placed strategically in the cloakroom and on the classroom door, e.g. 'Don't forget to say good morning!' or 'Let's begin today with a smile and a hello'. Help children to take ownership of remembering to greet both staff and peers. You will find some ready-made posters in the online resources for this book.

3   Make sure pupils notice the prompts and remember why they made them by pointing to the posters and indicating that they forgot something.

Your face as a resource

'It seems so unusual for children not to recognise facial expressions or pick up the emotion that is conveyed. I always thought this was a part of development for everyone.'

Understanding or reading facial expressions can be a real challenge for children with autism, but through using well-chosen resources and your own facial expression, you can provide a clear link to meaning.

In some ways, this is more than just failing to recognise the meaning behind facial expressions, as it can also result in misunderstanding and misinterpretation, leading to fear and anxiety. Like our discussion on greetings, many children need direct teaching to understand the subtleties of facial expression and body language.

Some of the most useful resources are not a drain on the school budget! For example:

- Use a 'teaching moment' to explain in context. If a child is crying from falling in the playground, point out that the child is sad and upset because he hurt his knee. Explain that tears show that we are sad. Similarly, if Azra is smiling, explain that she looks happy because it's her birthday.
- Use photos of real people to categorise into various facial or emotional expressions – sad, happy, excited, surprised, frightened, angry, etc. Help the children to recognise the subtle differences between some of the expressions.
- Use your face to model facial expressions and have the children imitate your look. Can they guess what you're trying to convey? Can they convey emotion through their face?

Ideas to support facial expression and gesture are provided in the online resources.

Taking it further

When expressions are recognised, begin to ask *why* the person looks that way. In the first instance, offer two or three pictures of contexts, one of which suits the facial expression. Eventually, help the children to come up with scenarios to explain why a person's face appears as it does.

Bonus idea ★

Take a look at the Consonantly Speaking website for great resources to support this area! http://www.consonantlyspeaking.com/

Playful opportunities

'It has been difficult to engage my children with autism in play and participation in social situations. I'd welcome any ideas to draw them in and see them enjoy sessions with the group.'

Making it fun to be part of a pair or group with creative and motivating resources can entice the child into social opportunities that lead to recognition of the role of others.

Teaching tip

Use YOUR imagination to heighten interest and enjoyment. Cast your inhibitions aside and delight your children! The online resources elaborate on opportunities to engage pupils in play.

By introducing play and active learning into your sessions, you will entice engagement and better enable participation. Try some of these ideas:

- Role play – link to provision areas and the dress-up corner.
- Puppets – to encourage conversation and emotions.
- Engaging resources – slime, gloop, balloons and bubbles.
- A treasure hunt to get everyone involved in finding artefacts for a new topic and then guessing what they represent.
- 'Awe' box – create a special box or container that becomes a regular occurrence to get attention. Make it sparkly, colourful or tactile to heighten interest. Introduce the box in a small group and conceal a special item that then gets passed around the group one at a time, each lifting the lid to peek at the object until everyone has had the experience – then disclose it and draw out vocabulary.
- Create dark, quiet and suspenseful spaces to tell a story and have the children 'chime' in with appropriate sounds – lightning and thunder, whispers and silence, or footsteps.
- Create expectation through sensory stories brought to life with the wind felt through a fan, the water through spray, the actual popping of a balloon or the rustle of leaves – lift the story off the page!

Peer support

'It worries me that a lot of the social opportunities I provide for Laura are with an adult. How do I help her relate to her peers?'

Children with autism often find social situations difficult and they can be doubly disadvantaged by being isolated from peers, even when we mean well. Using sensitive peers to help the child with autism participate, share and turn-take is immensely supportive in developing relationships and social awareness.

Let me be very clear: children on the autism spectrum cannot learn social skills in isolation. They have to be exposed to and involved with other children. A one-to-one session with an adult can coach the child to play a game but it then needs to be generalised to other contexts and other individuals.

1 Help children to understand winning and losing. It's okay to lose, and if this is an issue that causes high anxiety and tension, it will be difficult to play with peers.
2 Choose the peer group carefully to ensure that the experience will be positive.
3 Select activities that can be enjoyed by all with a reduction of competition. Encourage the children to compliment each other.
4 Use playtime to facilitate play with a small group: bubbles, chasing a balloon, etc.
5 Develop a 'buddy brigade' using children from the group to play with Laura outside and at wet play.

Peer support provides a positive experience for the child with autism. I observed an assembly where a child with autism sat next to a peer. The peer had a quiet symbol and when the child with autism began to make noise, his peer gently tapped the visual. On every occasion, the noise stopped and the peer gave a smile and a thumbs up. That's peer support!

Teaching tip

With parents' or carers' permission, explain why the pupils with autism find it difficult to socialise with others. By giving peers a better understanding, you are supporting the child with autism, raising awareness and preparing a group of children to recognise and accept diversity as they mature.

Extra-curricular opportunities

'We have quite a lot on offer at school but Kevin is so focused on his own interests that we can't get him to participate in clubs.'

In most schools, activities have been chosen because they are the things that children in the school enjoy. Consider looking at the special interests of specific children and develop a club around them. Other children could then be recruited to join this club.

I was in a school where a child was obsessed with a popular card game, and it was so disruptive to his learning that it was banned. The school started a lunchtime club, supporting the pupil and a group of peers to enjoy the game together – a win–win situation.

Consider *when* you are able to provide extra-curricular activities within your school. Will these be before school, after school, lunchtime, Friday afternoons, periodic Saturdays or holiday play schemes? The menu may include:

- rebound therapy to provide therapeutic exercise
- healthy snacks to share
- hairdressing salon
- computer challenge
- yoga
- table-top games
- Lego™
- art club
- green thumb garden.

Let the children suggest the focus; be creative about the titles and balance routine with variety. These opportunities provide development of social skills, cooperative ventures and life skills, expand experiences and enable children to try out new activities that may lead to future choices and interests. Further ideas and the positive impact they have on pupils are addressed in the online resources.

Mix it up

'Although Naomi is in my class group, she doesn't really relate to the peer group and needs some other opportunities to participate with a wider range of children. It isn't easy to solve this issue.'

It is not uncommon for children with autism to struggle in relating to peers. This can be the case in both special and mainstream schools. By considering the child's strengths and interests, a range of opportunities should be explored.

1 Look for opportunities to include Naomi in other groups within your school. They may be for a specific part of the curriculum where she shines and could join a group that would be at a similar achievement level, or where there is more peer interaction that would meet her needs.

2 Create a group to focus on a shared interest that would stimulate Naomi and others. It may be during teaching sessions or may be over lunchtime or after school. Is food an interest that could be motivating? Could the group create a flower bed and tend it? Remember to look for an activity where Naomi has the chance to interact, not just participate in parallel.

3 There will almost certainly be fewer females than males with autism in your school; consider whether developing a girls' group would be helpful. Depending on age, this may be to support hygiene and growing up.

4 Give careful consideration to whether Naomi, or other pupils in your school, would benefit from inclusion in a different local school. This may be a mainstream accessing a special school for targeted support such as communication and social skills, or it may be a special school accessing the local mainstream school for wider inclusion opportunities.

Teaching tip

You may have heard of 'Lego™ Therapy'. For some children, this provides a great opportunity to take a role alongside peers and develop skills that can be generalised to other contexts. The online resources provide examples of successful Lego™ Therapy sessions to heighten your interest.

Within the curriculum

'I try hard to use small groups and "talking partners" in my lesson planning but really struggle to engage Simon in any of this. He just doesn't seem to participate with the others.'

Look back at Part 4 and what has been discussed about the need for visual supports for your pupils with autism. If the main intention is for the children to talk together about a topic that may have been introduced verbally, it is not surprising that some children feel lost.

By the very nature of social communication being a difficulty for many children with autism, it is inevitable that a focus on pairs and group work will be a challenge. This is often an area where the deployment of staff is very important and can make the difference in whether the child will be able to participate or opt out.

Method 1 – Consider providing a staff facilitator for the group Simon is in; this will enable gentle guidance and the opportunity to ensure he has a voice within the group and that he is supported to communicate in his own way.

Method 2 – Carefully choose the peers that are paired with Simon or in the group with him. Do they understand his idiosyncrasies? Are they willing to accept and include rather than become impatient or critical?

Method 3 – Ensure that the individual communication needs are considered for Simon; should things be presented in symbols or in written form? Does he need a word bank or photographs to bring things to life for him?

Bonus idea ★

Nurture the group to the point where the peer group recognise and support Simon's needs and are sensitive to processing time, visual supports and the need for clarity. The skills you teach them now will benefit other children with autism whom they encounter in the years ahead.

Turn-taking techniques

'In my classroom, I often have the pupils play games where turn-taking is an important element. The game is ruined when Urooj jumps ahead of her turn. The other children get upset and we usually have to abandon the game completely. It doesn't seem fair.'

The temptation is to stop including children who don't yet understand turn-taking in games. In the end, this will not help the child or the others in the group. You need to consider what can be used to help them understand what turn-taking is.

Here are some things to try:

- a snap-on bracelet or finger puppet that is passed to the person taking the turn
- a wand that is pointed at the turn-taker
- a turn-taking wheel and arrow with names or photos to indicate whose turn it is
- use of the wait symbol to indicate waiting for your turn.

Always teach the skill of taking turns. Do not assume that it is known and understood. When a child has chosen to play in isolation and has been preoccupied with singular activities, it is not surprising that taking turns is a challenge. Taking turns involves waiting, paying attention to another person, and sharing time and resources. It requires sensitive introduction and pacing to avoid frustration. Taking turns on the computer, for example, will have to be facilitated in the first instance and supported visually with the tools indicated above. By using peers to model these skills and to provide positive examples, the child will be better equipped to understand the rules of the game.

Other ways to incorporate turn-taking through the day are provided in the online resources.

Bonus idea ★

Incorporate turn-taking throughout the day as a natural part of activities: in the playground, sharing resources, on the computer, interactive whiteboard, etc.

Thinking and saying

'Leroy is just rude. He's rude to me and he really upsets some of the other staff and children in school by the way he speaks to them. I can't just let him get away with it.'

It's so important to try to understand why a child may speak to you and others in a socially unacceptable way. Children with autism are literal thinkers and say what they see. They understand things from their own perspective and need to learn that we have to think before we speak.

Teaching tip

Try to see the comments from the perspective of the child rather than becoming offended. By using the insult as a teaching tool and helping the child to generalise an understanding about avoiding negative comments, you are helping to prepare for future relationships.

This visual tool can be helpful when addressing the difference between thinking and saying:

Method 1 – When Leroy gets it wrong, you will need to spend time to help him understand why he has upset someone. Take, for example, a child who said that he would not do his work and that the teacher was 'decidedly unattractive'! In his opinion, he was just being honest. He was too distracted to concentrate and listen in her lessons. By using the diagram above, it is possible for you to explain that it is okay to think something negative, but by vocalising it he was embarrassing his teacher and hurting her feelings. What could he have done instead? Often the answer for the 'What I say' bubble is 'nothing'. Teaching the idiom 'to bite your tongue' can be very helpful here. But it MUST be taught, or it may be taken literally, with painful results!

Method 2 – As hard as it may be, you need to have thick skin and never take insults personally. Deal with them in a matter-of-fact and calm way, trying to help Leroy to understand where he is getting it wrong. I worked with a child who, from the first day he joined our resource provision, told me, 'I don't like your grey hair, do something about it.' I calmly explained that it was my hair and I was happy with it being grey. This same conversation was repeated many times, and after a few weeks he gave me an exasperated look and said, 'You still have that grey hair but I guess it will be alright.' Making an issue of his opinion and setting up conflict would not have benefited either of us, and it would have been unacceptable for me to change my hair colour on demand!

A template to use and further examples of addressing this idea are available in the online resources.

> **Bonus idea** ★
>
> Prepare a selection of comment cards with both positive and negative statements referring to a person's appearance, characteristics and hygiene. Ask the child, or a small group of children, to categorise them into acceptable and non-acceptable comments. Establish understanding by discussing the rationale for the decisions.

Unstructured time unravels

'He finds the structure of the classroom so much easier than other times during the day. I need ways to improve the support across the school environment.'

The issue of unstructured time comes up over and over again. It's as if we remove the tried-and-tested supports when pupils close the classroom door behind them and then we wonder why things fall apart.

Let's think about what difficult times arise in the day. Typically, they are lunch, playtime, start of day and end of day. Most of your pupils look forward to these times of play and relaxation, when demands are fewer and enjoying time with friends is enabled. But for the child on the autism spectrum, these occasions increase anxiety, as the expectations to be social are heightened. Your pupil needs your support to navigate these unstructured times, and you can do this by:

- Recognising the need to provide visual support specific to the child – an object of reference, a mobile timetable or 'first/then'.
- Ensuring that all staff are aware of the child's apprehensions and proactively intervene if anxiety is heightening. Train auxiliary staff and use them to facilitate social communication between children.
- Using peers to invite the child to participate and to engage with the interests of the child. Ask for volunteers who are willing to take a turn to do this during the week.
- Providing a small group to join the child at the dinner table. Consider organising conversation topics to draw social responses from the child. Make this a time to encourage sharing special interests. If staffing is available, provide a member of staff to encourage the flow of conversation.

Developing independence

Part 6

Challenge v. reassurance

'Our school has a good ratio of support for children on the autism spectrum but I sometimes worry that there is too much adult input.'

It comes naturally to adults in the caring professions to reassure and nurture, but it is necessary to find the balance between supporting and challenging the child in order to develop independence.

I'm sure you have heard the phrase 'the staff seem to be stuck to the child' or 'she seems to be joined at the hip with that pupil'. I often think that when a member of staff is appointed to support a pupil one to one, they feel guilty if every minute of the day is not spent overseeing, prompting, organising and caring for the pupil. How does this affect the development of independence for the child? Clearly it impedes progress in this area.

It is so important to remember that staff are not personal assistants to the pupils but are there to help each child to develop into a responsible and independent individual. The role is NOT to wrap the pupil in cotton wool but to challenge, encourage, enable and celebrate the successes as they unfold.

Stop and consider:

- Who takes the child's coat off and hangs it on the peg?
- Who carries his lunch tray?
- Who peels her banana?
- Who sharpens his pencil?
- Who gets out the resources the pupil needs?
- Who buttons and zips his jacket?

There are so many little things throughout the day where staff need to respect and encourage pupils to act independently. Balance the development of skills with the need to oversee and support.

Bonus idea ★

Develop an open climate in your school where staff are invited to draw attention to situations where a colleague fails to notice an opportunity to enable independence. It is so easy to miss where we go wrong if we are not observed objectively by someone else.

Home–school liaison

'I was taken by surprise when I discovered that things Carl was doing independently at school required help at home. Why the inconsistency?'

If an element of independence is achieved at school but NOT linked with the same skills at home, it will not have a long-lasting effect. The reverse is also true; if a pupil is showing independence at home but the same skills are requiring help at school, consistency needs to be addressed.

Many scenarios are often raised in this area. For example, in the school routine, Carl dresses and undresses for PE with minimal support but at home his parents report that he sits passively and expects them to dress him. In all probability, the situation at home reflects the routine that was first established when the child was younger. Because it is the routine, both he and his parents have continued it. At school, a visual schedule has been introduced and, by following it, the pupil can (with minimal staff prompts) dress and undress independently.

In the first instance, the schedule will be prompted by staff to encourage the pupil to understand the steps. Then prompting will be diminished and the child will be encouraged to follow independently. But if this is happening successfully at school, then the schedule needs to be shared with and explained to parents. Being consistent with the strategy and its presentation will make it possible for the child to transfer the skill to home and to begin to do things for himself. Bed-time routine can be added, as can schedules for brushing teeth, washing hands, gathering things for his school bag, etc. All of these things are life skills, and the earlier they are introduced and established, the better it is for the future of independent living.

Taking it further

Ensure that liaison with family/carers is strong, and work together to support consistency and ensure that the child is challenged to succeed in both environments. Guidelines and helpful ideas to support liaison with parents are provided in the online resources.

Stand back and shadow

'I'm the teacher. I should take charge. I don't want anything to go wrong but sometimes I realise I step in too quickly and inhibit the pupils from having a go.'

Adults often feel the need to be in charge. Not only do we want to help but we also want to prevent mistakes and mishaps. By intervening too quickly, we deprive the children of practising new skills and learning from their mistakes.

Taking it further

When setting targets for pupils, always include specific ones focusing on independence. For example, 'To find the correct materials for my session and organise them on my desk' or 'To store my coat and bag on the correct hook in the cloakroom'. This is not an optional extra but an essential part of planning for progress.

Throughout the day, there are multiple opportunities to facilitate independence and empower your children to take responsibility. Too often, as the child walks through the school door, a well-meaning member of staff relieves them of the school bag and carries it to the classroom. This is often followed by hanging the coat on the peg and shepherding the child to their seat. No, no, no! Stand back, enable the child to take ownership of belongings and only intervene if a difficulty arises, such as a stuck zipper or too much to carry on a given day. When support is needed, use it as an opportunity to develop communication, and encourage the child to ask you for help and to indicate what the problem is.

In some respects, this is a mind shift. You need to move from feeling guilty about not waiting on the children in your care to feeling robust about the need for you to be an integral part of preparing them for the future – for confidence, independence and responsibility. By exercising discernment and patience, you will be making a positive difference that will reap benefits for years to come.

A list of targets to support independence is provided in the online resources.

Promote problem solving

'I worry that I step in too early sometimes and don't give Robert the time he needs to process a problem before I solve it for him. I think I worry that pushing independence causes him anxiety and I avoid that at all costs!'

Judging when to intervene or step back and wait is a valid concern. From the earliest opportunity, however, finding ways to encourage problem solving is a necessity and is the forerunner to establishing life skills that are an essential foundation for future development.

I saw an excellent example of a teacher promoting problem solving not long ago. A youngster was trying to exit the classroom into the play area and had forgotten that there was a door release to the right of the door. The teacher did not remind him what to do nor did she push the release for him. She waited, gestured and said, 'Oh dear, how do we get out?' She waited, 'eye-pointed' to the release and he caught on. He pushed the release and away he went. It took a little longer but he did it himself. He solved the problem with support and will almost certainly remember the next time.

Staff mean well and want to help, but in so doing neglect to recognise that children need to learn to solve problems. By asking questions rather than giving answers, by gesturing rather than taking over and by waiting rather than rushing in, you are supporting children to think through and be successful in solving their own problems.

Teaching tip

Use 'Sabotage!' (Idea 76) as a creative way to set up a problem to encourage solutions by the children. Questions such as, 'What's missing and what can we use instead?' encourage flexible thought. Scenarios describing how to move from intervening to enabling are provided in the online resources.

Generalising understanding

'Sometimes I get confused when Ashley has seemed to understand something well and then shows confusion when the same thing is presented slightly differently.'

Most of your children will be able to generalise or transfer their learning from one situation to another, while some will become confused when the context changes.

Consider a couple of examples:

1 David was taught to measure accurately in maths. When he was handed a ruler in art to draw a cube, he sat without working until the teacher asked him what was wrong. He said he didn't know how to measure without a ruler. The teacher pointed out that he had a ruler and David was even more confused. The issue? The ruler in maths had been plastic. The ruler in art was wooden. The teacher found a plastic ruler and showed the two together, explaining that they were both rulers but made from different materials. He pointed out the lines and numbers and helped David to generalise the term 'ruler'.

2 Mason struggled with inappropriate touching of female staff. Through discussion and rules being established, this behaviour had stopped completely. He then began integration at a mainstream school and the behaviour began in the new setting. Concerns were raised. When asked why, he explained, 'Oh, I thought you just meant at this school. I didn't know you meant there.' Needless to say, further explanations took place and the understanding was generalised to **all** settings.

The onus is on you to recognise an issue of generalisation and then take the time to explain the links. Your diligence in this area will open up new opportunities and help your children to broaden their perspectives.

Organising for success

'Victoria gets easily frustrated with resources when she's working, often ending in her pushing things away and refusing to continue.'

When difficulties with resources arise, they may indicate an issue with 'executive function'. This refers to skills that include organising, regulating, working, impulse and attention. The child may need additional support and carefully planned tasks to achieve success. The other problem may be that the child is struggling to cope with the way in which tasks are presented.

There are times when we produce resources that are creative and perfect for developing learning but we inadvertently make them unmanageable. For example, laminating matching games is great, but if the materials slide away and have to be replaced whenever there is a bit of movement, the task ends up on the floor. Providing Velcro™ or another removable adhesive that stabilises the pieces makes it manageable and reduces frustration. A container for pencils and felt tips, rather than loose ones rolling off the desk, and clearly labelled resources that are readily accessible enable independence and, in turn, bolster confidence with getting on with a task.

An important aspect of task organisation is storage and putting things away. This should be a responsibility given to the child. There are many options for storing resources to ensure that they are maintained well and that components are not lost, e.g. zip bags, boxes, plastic containers and wallets. Part of putting things away is checking that everything is gathered together. This skill, generalised, makes for an orderly classroom and has positive implications for family life as well.

Teaching tip

Using a range of containers also helps to develop the skills of doing and undoing fasteners and zips, which are skills required for independent dressing.

Taking it further

Learn more about executive function by referring to information included in the further reading on page 124. Supportive ideas to enable success are outlined in the online resources.

Pupil voice

'Trying to get it right for non-verbal children in my group is such a challenge. I want to help them communicate and express their opinions.'

When communication is one of the main challenges for children on the autism spectrum, it is too easy for the adults to assume that the child is unable to express opinions. Finding creative solutions to enable the pupils to have a voice is a challenge that reaps benefits for pupils and staff alike.

One of the challenges of working with children on the autism spectrum is enabling the child to communicate needs, wants, likes, dislikes, fears, preferences and opinions. Too often, the adult makes the choices, with the best intentions, of course!

Through asking the right questions and enabling through verbal and/or visual prompts, staff can facilitate children to identify when they are having a good or bad day, ways to help when stress is rising, things that are causing worry and things that are making it difficult to concentrate.

But finding appropriate ways to empower the child to have that voice is so very important. Take, for example, a child being asked to identify aspects of the curriculum that are liked or disliked. Here is one of the ways you could approach this challenge:

1 Provide a like/dislike table or chart.

☺ I like	☹ I do not like

2 Provide photographs, symbols or words to depict your focus. For example, trying to find out how the child feels about different areas of the curriculum:
📖 ✎ ❶❷❸ 🖥 ♪

3 The child then places the symbol on the side of the table that relates to the response given.

4 This same approach can be used to find favoured activities, foods, safe places in school, etc. Using a wide range of photographs or symbols will offer the best outcomes.

In an observation of this scenario, a teacher was surprised to see art under the sad face. When she attempted to find out why, the child showed her the paint overall with the elasticated wrists, indicating that it was too tight. It wasn't art he disliked – it was the overall! This was an easy problem to solve, but it could have been totally missed and interpreted as being the subject (art) that he disliked if he threw the overall to the floor and was not given the opportunity to communicate his opinion. This model can be adapted to any context where information is being sought.

Similarly, a choice board depicting activities can enable the child to indicate preferences. Developing the choice board from the favoured activities identified by the child through the like/dislike strategy on the previous page will give the choice board value. The Picture Exchange Communication System® (PECS) follows the same principle by providing photographs or symbols for the child to choose and request from an adult. This system enhances the pupil voice by, for example, choosing not just a biscuit but a chocolate biscuit, not just a crayon but the colour of the crayon.

Enabling pupils to have a voice empowers them to advocate for themselves, and to build confidence, self-esteem and resilience. Discussion on being sensitive to and enabling pupils to express themselves is presented in the online resources.

Taking it further

Check out Talking Mats® and Talking Mats Digital – an interactive communication tool: http://www.talkingmats.com/

Please show me how

'Sometimes my teacher thinks I understand what I have to do but I just sit there because I didn't understand what she said. I just wish she'd show me how and then I could follow her example.'

Not understanding what is being expected can be further complicated by the child's reluctance to ask for support. As you are not a mind-reader, there ends up being frustration on both sides.

It may be helpful to think of the many times we, as adults, benefit from having someone alongside us to help us learn something new. For example, we often learn new technology through demonstration and/or one-to-one tuition. You may even write down notes to help you retain what it is you're learning so that you can refer back to it later. We're all familiar with the phrase 'here's one I made earlier'. The physical model of an idea takes us beyond words to a clearer understanding.

If we fail to understand an instruction, we begin to panic, and the higher the anxiety becomes, the less likely we are to be able to follow the instruction. For many children, this may result in shutting down or losing control. This is not in any way supporting independence. Recognising the need to demonstrate, to instruct through visuals and to provide individual explanations is essential.

'Showing me' is not just for model-making. It is essential in introducing any new skill. This may be using a new art material, such as charcoal or pastels, or it may be introducing the use of an index or a thesaurus. Preparing through *showing* is important – a little extra time, a few more demonstrations and reinforcement can make all the difference!

In the community

'We try to take our pupils into the community to expand their horizons. Concerns about risks seem to overtake developing independence. How can we improve our strategies?'

Concerns about risk and health and safety are understandable. Well-planned visits to local amenities and trips further afield can be an excellent way to develop independence and life skills.

Learning about money in the classroom (please use real coins rather than plastic) is a necessary part of the curriculum, but the shop set up in the corner of the classroom does not replace the local shop, where real choices and transactions can be made. The additional skills of confidence to communicate with the shopkeeper, safety while walking and crossing roads, using a shopping list and managing money in a purse all add to life skills and independence.

Some schools have the benefit of their own swimming pool and sports halls but as children move through the Key Stages, using the facilities in the local community supports the child to be able to navigate public spaces. An added benefit is making it possible for parents and carers to use local venues as a family, knowing that their child is familiar with the setting.

The balance of risk must always be considered. Risk assessments must be carefully planned in advance. Linking community opportunities to the curriculum and the targets of the children should be an integral part of the planning. Vocabulary development, observations, introducing new experiences and exposing children to the wider world are all enhanced through community involvement. Bringing topics to life for your pupils is not only worth the planning but is instrumental to their growth and development.

Teaching tip

Raising awareness in the community is an important aspect of supporting children on the autism spectrum. See the online resources for ideas to support this.

Bonus idea

You are doing a great service to the parents/carers of your pupils by introducing them to a variety of experiences and helping their children to cope in new and varied environments. This, in turn, will enable families to access community venues and improve family life.

Curriculum focus

'Elise is very capable in her work but has such a struggle having the confidence to work independently.'

Struggling to work independently despite academic success is not uncommon, and there are a range of ways to help pupils gain greater independence as they tackle curriculum work.

Teaching tip

Other issues arise in the curriculum that can create anxiety for the child and prevent getting on with the task at hand. One of these is the stress brought on by making an error and wanting the written work to be perfect. This can result in the work being torn up and rejected for one spelling mistake or wrong word. Never belittle the situation. A Social Story™ can be helpful here; explain that it is okay to make mistakes and that a line through the work is acceptable. See the online resources for further information.

Taking it further

The online resources provide ideas about broadening horizons across the curriculum.

In one group I worked with, a target was set by each pupil and displayed on the corner of their desk. One of the girls had a tendency to daydream rather than work, and when we chatted about a target that might help her, she came up 'Just keep on working!'. It was there to remind her, but if I noticed the distraction I would just walk past her table and gently tap on the target, bringing her back to the task at hand.

Supporting curriculum tasks needs to take into account the individual needs of the pupils. Remember that there may be areas of strength where the work is easily accepted and completed with little intervention. In areas where extra organisation is required, consider:

- Written step-by-step instructions.
- Providing a word bank to support the necessary vocabulary.
- Reducing the amount of written work if fine motor issues are present.
- Diagrams or photographs to heighten understanding and interest.
- Scaffolding – breaking the learning into chunks and providing structure.
- Well-prepared resources that are manageable for the child's organisation and the space available.
- Peer support to keep on task.
- Reducing distractions in the environment.
- Making clear the time available for the task and when it ends.

Differentiation matters

Part 7

Clearly defined

'I had become used to differentiating for groups but discovered that I really needed to look at each of my ASD children as an individual – what a challenge!'

Given that each child is unique, it is imperative that differentiation is fit for the specific needs, learning style and ability of the individual.

Teaching tip

One of the most exciting and fulfilling things you can do is to develop bespoke activities and presentations of tasks to meet differentiated needs.

This is a big ask, isn't it? Whether you are teaching in a mainstream school, with one or two children with autism in your class group, or in a special school, where your entire group is on the autism spectrum, differentiating the content, resources and approach is the challenge you face.

Let's imagine that you are introducing a topic on the senses. Some of your children will be able to respond to each with a clear understanding from experience. But for children who do not readily learn through osmosis, there is a need to bring the senses to life in a creative way. You can't just talk about taste; the children need to experience it. You can't just 'imagine' how something feels; your children need to touch. Photos of woolly blankets, sponges, glass paper and pot scrubbers are fine for some to categorise, but may not be enough for children who need concrete experiences.

Consider how much work is expected. Does each child have to accomplish the same thing? Is writing out in sentences essential for comprehension or can cut and paste or highlighting show understanding? Making concrete resources available for maths, additional visuals to support literacy, adapted seating, pencil grips, work stations, short breaks, etc. are all part of differentiation.

Here's one I created earlier

'The rest of the group get fired up when we are tackling a creative project but Matias seems lost and has no idea where to begin. How can I help him to invent something of his own?'

Not everyone can conjure up an imaginative idea. Having a model of what is expected enables the child to *see* what you are asking. A range of models is even better, as it provides choice.

Modelling is an effective way of helping pupils to understand what is expected of them. However, if you merely show one model, there is a danger that the pupil will copy that exactly and not contribute any of their own ideas. They will need to be helped to expand, alter and extend. One way to do this is to offer the pupil choices in a way in which they can access them, e.g. verbally, with a choice board or using concrete objects. Initially, you may demonstrate through a black and white drawing that you want the children to develop into a colourful 3D model. This brings in many choices of materials, adhesives, colours and mediums. Making the options available for the pupil to choose from, rather than request, adds to the visual support provided.

Skills will also need to be taught to pupils if new materials and mediums are to be used. Use some of their peers to demonstrate as they develop their own piece of work. Experiment with some of the resources on offer before they are applied to the final product. Encourage and praise the pupil as they venture into something new and different.

Do remember that pupils may find it very difficult to create an imaginary object/creature/model. Give them some leeway to master the skills needed and use the resources provided to produce a more standard product that they can be proud of and showcase to others.

Bonus idea ★

Help the pupil to create a fun gathering project like a mind map. Explore colours, shapes, textures, images, photos, resources, etc. This will set the scene for creating something unique and original.

Use *your* imagination

'As an experienced teacher, I have never had to work so hard to engage some of the pupils in my class. The wheels of my brain are constantly turning.'

Creativity is one of the most essential characteristics for working with children with autism. Given that one of the common challenges for children with ASD is the area of 'imagination', recognising this and creatively using *your* imagination to plan effectively and provide appropriate support is a must.

You are probably familiar with the idea that if a child does not learn from the way we teach, we need to teach in the way the child will learn. That's really what this book is all about. You, as a teacher, need to find the pathway that taps into and arouses the child's learning. No small task! Let's think about some ideas.

Dean struggles with fine motor movements and needs to develop the pincer grip to strengthen his fingers. Pencils and crayons alone will not turn him into a writer with pace. Developing fun activities such as using clothes pegs and tweezers to pick up small objects, threading small beads or pushing sticks or pipe cleaners into a water bottle – all fun to do – will improve fine motor skills. A creative occupational therapist made a bespoke threading idea for one of our pupils by fixing a smiling snake head to a flexible wire, with each spool wrapped with a different texture to create interest and tactile experiences – a real motivator. Using plastic tweezers to move small objects from a bowl to an empty water bottle is helpful for both fine motor and eye–hand coordination. Choose a variety of shapes and sparkly objects to inject interest.

Remember that many of your pupils with autism need concrete learning experiences, and not just 2D paper presentation. Most of your children could look at photos of things made from different materials – wood, plastic, glass, fabric, metal. For some, however, you need to provide an array of real objects made from these materials and let the children *experience* the feel, the texture and the pliability. They then need to compare them to other things around the room made of the same substance and categorise them accordingly. Only then will the photographs or drawings begin to make sense, and matching against them will bring understanding.

To heighten imagination:

- Create attractive, stimulating, bespoke resources.
- Use the child's special interest and expand on it, e.g. can the super hero rescue a classmate, use a new phrase or solve a problem?
- Engage the child in pretend play such as dressing up, tea party, post office, etc.

Taking it further

If the child does not recognise the intention of a toy, help to develop this understanding. If the bicycle is turned on its side and the wheels spun, support the child to ride the bicycle; if building bricks are always used in the same colour pattern, provide visuals to show and encourage variety, etc.

Homework hassles

'Luke is quite biddable in school and tries his best right across the curriculum. When it comes to homework, he is resistant and makes it very difficult for his parents. We are working together to try to find solutions but not successfully.'

Homework is a problem that comes up over and over again. One issue is related to the clear separation that many children make between home and school. If this is school work, why do I have to do it at home? This idea offers advice about how to explain the purpose of homework to your children.

Taking it further

Homework must be provided in visual or written form. This may be in the pupil's school diary, in a home–school book, by email to parents or by text to the child. It is important to choose the format to best suit the pupil and help him/her to have ownership of the work.

Differentiation really is important when it comes to homework – not only in the way the work is assigned, in keeping with the differentiation of the curriculum within the classroom, but also in the quantity and insistence on where it is done. Many children with autism find it hard to accept that school intrudes on home life. They see the time outside of school as personal and family time and resent the intrusion of the teacher deciding what they should do in that space.

A couple of options to consider:

1 Is it necessary that the work has to be done at home? Consider a lunchtime club or after-school club where support can be provided for this work. Can the school be flexible enough to offer this to pupils with autism and other peers who may prefer this? Remember that some children on the autism spectrum do not enjoy the unstructured time of breaks and play and may be very happy to have this option.
2 Explain the reason for homework to the child and help them to understand the reason for it and the amount of time expected. The diagram on the next page may be helpful.

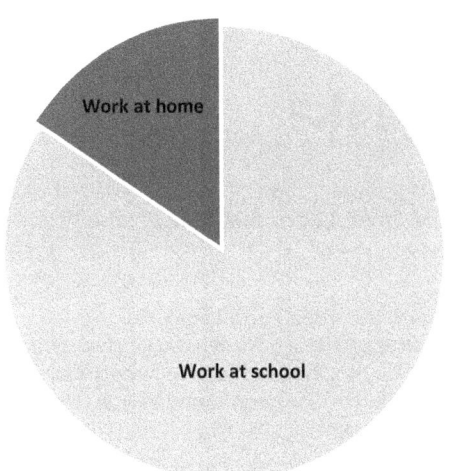

Work at home

Work at school

It demonstrates that the vast majority of work is done at school and only a small portion is at home.

3 Help the home to set up an after-school schedule, so that the pupil understands that they can still enjoy the family and home activities. For example, they could have a break when arriving home, do homework and then go back to relaxation.

Building in breaks

'Jenny seems to find it difficult to stay focused for as long as her peer group and gets very restless at times. I don't feel I can excuse her from her work and expect everyone else to carry on.'

For many children with autism, the need for a break during times of work and the challenge of sitting for a long period and becoming restless is a real issue. Pupils need *you* to recognise the saturation point and offer them – or help them to ask for – a break; this is a reasonable adjustment.

Teaching tip

If it is difficult for the child to request a break, try providing an 'I need a break' card that they can bring to you.

Firstly, you need to recognise the signs that pupils show when they are reaching the point of going off task or becoming agitated. For some children, the very nature of being in a busy classroom is overwhelming, and a break may be necessary to enable refocus. Helping the child to recognise heightened anxiety and ask for a break promotes the child's understanding and develops independence. It may be a subtle gesture that has been decided upon between the two of you, or it may be a visual prompt on the child's table or a 'pass' to give you when required.

Let's think of some ways in which you can recognise when a pupil needs a break and offer one in a natural way. For example, you can send the pupil to the office with a message – the message may be a note asking the receptionist to initiate a short conversation with them, to support their social and communication targets. Some breaks are natural, such as morning play, refilling a water bottle, dinner time and movement to the hall or specialist rooms. These times of transition provide both a change of position and exercise.

In schools, we are very group-orientated and often fail to recognise the overwhelming pressure that this puts on children who do not easily relate to their peers or assimilate into the classroom environment. Providing a more varied schedule to take this into account can be very beneficial for children with autism.

Consider, for example, times when the class is working in small groups. It is inevitable that the volume rises, and this may be a trigger of anxiety for children with autism who are distracted by peripheral noise. Be creative about reducing the impact. You may have the group that the child is in work outside the class area in a quieter location, where the voices are reduced to five or six voices rather than 30. You may offer ear defenders if the issue is one of a sensory nature. You may recognise that the ability to cope is limited and offer short breaks away from the setting at appropriate intervals. A sand timer may make this more manageable.

Do respect the fact that some children need a bit of time to regain focus and composure, and make this a natural part of the day rather than a time of confrontation or disruption.

Taking it further

Make any break purposeful. For example, give the pupil some responsibility, such as gathering the recyclables from the classroom to deliver to the gathering point in school, or have responsibility for watering plants, tidying the book corner or sharpening pencils. The task may be a set time that you have identified as 'breaking point' or it may be flexible, when you or the pupil recognises the need for a break.

These are a few of my favourite things

'Martin's limited interests make it difficult to engage him in the curriculum I need to cover. How can I turn this round?'

Many children with autism have special interests – particular things that they focus on and enjoy. Rather than struggle with the preoccupation, consider how you can make use of it to enhance and entice the child to learn.

By using the special interest as a reward to be enjoyed following the completion of tasks during the day, you are respecting the pupil's interests and helping them to focus on your agenda. For some children, it is a challenge to put their own fascination on hold, and by being creative (there's that word again!) you can use the special interest to tap into learning across the curriculum.

Take, for example, an obsessive interest in trains. Here are some ways in which you could include trains in your curriculum:

- Maths: time, timetables, distance, speed, ticket cost, cost to run.
- Geography: types of trains in different countries, routes, terrain, maps.
- History: development of steam engine, diesel, electric, use in the past/present.
- Literacy: story of a journey, facts, famous trains report, alphabetical order of stations.
- Science: pros and cons of energy use, types of engines and fuels, impact on the environment.

By combining the special interest as an incentive for completing work, and by allowing a measure of flexibility in how to cover the curriculum, you will be respecting the individual needs of your pupil but not sacrificing the learning goals. Sometimes we are guilty of being more inflexible than our pupils!

Engaging resources

'I am learning that Amal does not respond to worksheets and written tasks. She needs a different approach to be engaged and to stay focused. Any ideas?'

There are many ways to offer alternatives to worksheets. Some schools are well resourced for learning activities and are able to provide a selection of motivating games and activities. Many of the commercially produced items can be replicated by you to meet your pupil's needs, even when budgets are tight.

The first thing you need to consider is the learning intent of the task. I have seen many tedious, time-consuming written tasks that involve writing out sentences, even though the focus is on comprehension and not on penmanship. Could the child be given the sentences and join the correct answer to a choice of words? Could they write the one required word rather than the sentence? The worry is that some worksheets are for the purpose of filling in time – you need to guard against this.

Memory games are wonderful for developing concentration, turn-taking and curriculum skills. Rather than a worksheet with addition and subtraction sums, for example, a memory game is an interactive way to demonstrate understanding and work with peers at the same time. In the example to the right, the individual cards are turned upside down and selected two at a time. The goal is to find the matching pair, e.g. 7+2 and 9. Bingo can also be used for a wide range of skills in an engaging way. The learning goal can be achieved and evidenced in an active way.

The online resources provide links to helpful resources.

Teaching tip

I'm sure one of your concerns will be the time it takes to develop your own resources. Is it possible for you to recruit a parent or grandparent volunteer to be your assistant in this area? Having someone to carry out your ideas will bring them to fruition.

7+2	5+5	6
5	1+5	4+3
7	3+2	3
0+3	10	9

Generate generalisation

'Just when I think I have explained things fully and have consolidated the learning, Lesley looks blank and I realise the new context has thrown her completely.'

When children fail to make the links between one context and another, it is imperative that you recognise the problem and are sensitive to how you can bridge the gap and help the child begin to generalise understanding.

Taking it further

Generalising skills between home and school can be a stumbling block. Work closely with parents for mutual support. One child sat beautifully at the dinner table at school but only ate in the lounge at home, in spite of his parents' efforts to sit together as a family. School used a laminated placemat with the child's name and an outline of plate, cutlery and glass. Making an identical placemat to take home helped in changing the arrangements at home and encouraging generalising to other eating contexts.

It may sound strange, but I'm always really pleased when teachers realise how important context is! Doing so means you are showing that you are sensitive to pupils' misunderstandings, and that means you will help them to generalise new skills. We so readily take for granted that when we teach a skill it is transferred to new contexts by the children we work with. When this is not the case, we are caught short and, actually, this provides a wonderful learning opportunity for you as the teacher!

Lesley may have learned about liquid measure in science, but when the skill was needed in a new context – the food technology room – the container was different and confusion ensued. Explaining that the different receptacles have the same demarcation on the sides and are used in the same way will help Lesley to generalise the skill. Gather other varieties of containers to explain the concept further.

We use so many different terms and, once again, expect that Lesley and others will automatically understand them. Maths is a good example of this. Think about 'add, plus, sum, total, and' – we use these terms interchangeably. Having a visual prompt to link the words and the symbol provides clarity. Pertinent examples of the difficulties in this area are provided in the online resources.

Addressing the curriculum

'Beth is ahead of the group in maths and so focused during those sessions. Her reading has really come on but comprehension is an incredible challenge. She just doesn't pay attention.'

Some pupils have what is often referred to as a 'spiky profile', which baffles many teachers. Why, you ask, can a pupil do so well in one area and struggle in another?

One of the explanations for a spiky profile is that, in the case mentioned above, Beth gets the logic of maths. 2+2 is always 4, while there is no absolute in many areas such as literacy, social studies and the arts. Reading is sometimes very strong because it is decoding – making logical sense of the way letters go together to make words. But decoding is very different from comprehending the content of a text, and results in reading without meaning.

Understanding this should help you recognise that Beth has great ability but needs to be supported in different ways across different subjects. It's important to remember that the ease of solving numerical problems can become difficult when they become word problems and Beth has to comprehend the text.

Help Beth to recognise that she can be successful in comprehension by teaching her the skill to look back at the written information to find the answer. For example, rather than asking her, 'What was the teacher explaining to the class in the passage we just read?', instruct her to find the sentence where the teacher was explaining things to the class and identify the answer. You are testing her comprehension but assisting her in how to isolate the information she needs.

Teaching tip

When you have identified strengths and weaknesses, build on the former to support the latter and always affirm success. The online resources address the issues presented by the 'spiky profile' that some ASD pupils experience.

Outside the classroom

'We are trying to find new ways to take learning outside the traditional classroom context.'

It's so exciting when the curriculum becomes part of a wider dynamic than enclosed walls. I have observed some amazingly innovative approaches that draw children into learning.

The Forest School movement is expanding and brings to life new environments and life skills that captivate pupils' imaginations. Experiencing the outdoors, and learning about plants, forest birds and creatures, navigation and exploring, raises confidence and creates new interests.

Some schools have developed outdoor classrooms linked with horticulture and innovative mini-enterprise projects. For example, one group of children developed a weekly staff sandwich menu, taking orders in advance, making a shopping list, buying the ingredients, making and delivering on the day. The book-keeping was meticulous and they voted on how to spend the profits. Sometimes they chose to go out for lunch together, requiring further collaborative and investigative work to agree on a restaurant, transportation and budget. Such activities tick the boxes for learning, independence, peer-engagement and confidence-building – wins all round.

Using the local community for access to leisure and shopping builds foundations for independence in adulthood. Visits to cafes and restaurants use literacy through reading the menu, courtesy through table manners, speaking through ordering and table conversation, maths through calculating what is spent and ensuring there is enough money, plus exchanging money for payment, safe use of public toilets, etc.

Motivation inspires

Part 8

Target the praise

'I've struggled to understand why Jayden ignores me when I praise him. He doesn't seem to recognise or care about my compliments.'

We too often give praise through comments such as 'well done' and 'good for you' without attaching meaning to the words. What has been well done? What is good for me?

When giving praise, try to be specific and name what it is that you are pleased with. 'Good listening', 'Your drawing is lovely' or 'I like the way you coloured the picture' all explain what the praise is for. We may fall into the trap of commenting on the person by saying 'good boy' or 'good girl' without directing the focus to what the positive behaviour is. By labelling the action – for example, 'Thank you for tidying the book corner, that was very helpful' or 'Well done, you stopped as soon as I asked you to' – you are pointing out the actions that result in the compliment.

When we make reference to the 'goodness' of the child, we too often fall into the trap of using negative labels as well – bad and naughty. Weighing our words carefully leads to clearer communication, affirming the efforts and success of children and helping them to want to do the job well again next time. We, as adults, also like to be told what we do well. We all thrive on positive feedback and praise. Let's remember this when we acknowledge the attempts that our children make and the small steps they may achieve.

WOW wall

'I'm trying to create a positive and affirming atmosphere in the classroom but sometimes feel like my enthusiasm is lost on the pupils. Any ideas?'

We've talked a lot about verbal as compared to visual communication, and while it's wonderful to vocalise and share your zeal for a job well done, making it concrete is even better. Capture the moments when positive things happen and give them permanence by posting them on a reserved space in the room.

I've seen this used to great effect in some classrooms. Sometimes it's through the use of sticky notes that get written quickly and posted in a reserved space. Sometimes the comments are written on bronze, silver and gold celebration shapes. The positive comments record the child's name and the reason for the 'wow'. It may be a piece of work, contribution to discussion, an act of kindness to a peer, a new skill – the options are limitless. What a wonderful way to celebrate the success of children in a spontaneous way throughout the day. Consider these positive comments and their impact on the child:

- Ali greeted Liam with a lovely hello this morning.
- Martin played a game with two friends at break.
- Lisa shared her tablet with Damian.
- Alejandro spelled every word correctly on his test.
- Jenny helped to tidy up the classroom after the art and craft session.
- Mateo took a message to the office by himself.

A strategy such as this helps us to look for the positives and to offer incentives to every child in the group – opportunities to be affirmed and acknowledged.

Teaching tip

You may consider letting the children nominate peers for the 'wow' wall as well – they sometimes recognise things that we don't notice.

Taking it further

This is a lovely display for parents to see when they visit the classroom. Sharing the 'wows' through the home–school book or sending a duplicate home will encourage parents/carers to join in the celebration.

Session appraisal

'I realise it's important to get the pupils' opinions on how a session has gone, but when communication is a difficulty it is very hard to know how they can express themselves.'

This is a very real issue. We may think a session went very well — but what is the child's perspective? Find a way to elicit information through a child-friendly response.

Taking it further

Don't limit the session appraisal to like or dislike. Enable the children to choose what they enjoyed most about the session – this may be through a slideshow of options or by the concrete presence of activities that have been provided.

Helping children to develop a recognisable and valid way to offer their opinions can prove difficult. Tokenistic systems that have value for you but no real meaning for your pupils will not elicit the opinions you want.

I have seen some excellent self-appraisal tools used in classrooms, where their value was shown on the facial expressions of the pupils – for example, a plenary that was presented as a slideshow, pausing to show the children participating and giving them the opportunity to touch ✓ or ✗ on the screen to indicate whether they liked or disliked the activity. Other ideas are to reflect back through, showing the finished work and having children indicate with thumbs up 👍 or down 👎. Emoji faces are commonly used to indicate response: ☺ ☹. A shake of the head, a smile or a photo of the joy during the session all help you to assess the success of the lesson. Don't forget to give the children the opportunity to respond verbally if this is possible for them.

Do remember that for any of these symbols to be used effectively, they have to be understood by the children. This will mean that you will reinforce their meaning. An example could be providing opportunities for the child to comment on favoured activities, as you know whether the relevant symbol is correct and can affirm this: 'Yes, you do like Lego™, don't you?' while showing the ✓ or ☺ or 👍 to accompany.

Self-appraisal

'Ayra has begun to comment on the sessions and how she has enjoyed them. I'm trying to help her to comment on how she has done, and whether she has finished her work and been successful. This is presenting a new struggle.'

Self-appraisal is such a difficult area and yet so important for helping pupils to understand what their targets are and whether they are able to meet them.

Of course, the first thing is to make sure that the pupil knows what is expected of them in the session. The task or activity must be clear. This is discussed in the topic on visuals, where the importance of making the target child-friendly is explained (Idea 33). If the pupil is to complete 15 number bonds, does this correctly and is then asked to evaluate their work, it seems straightforward that they will give themselves a positive comment. If the task is to draw a still life picture, there is more subjectivity, but the pupils can still evaluate their efforts.

Taking it further

Ensure that the child's targets are clearly understood and presented visually. An example can be found in the online resources for this book.

Symbols work here as well, but a middle-of-the-road choice is often helpful: ☺. One school I visited used the terms 'EPIC' ☺, 'GOOD' ✎ and 'NEED MORE PRACTICE' ☺. The pupils were realistic in their assessments and none of the responses were seen as negative. Stars, number ratings and colour-coding can be used by the children to show how they feel they have done in their work. Helping them to recognise their own success is a step towards setting personal goals and further developing independence in achieving success.

That's me – display to celebrate

'The first time I did a photo display of a topic we were working on, I discovered that Katie and Andreas could hardly take their eyes off it. I realised how important the inclusion of people and not just work was to draw them in.'

Capturing events and expressions through digital photography is common classroom practice, and using these personal images in display brings meaning and a sense of identity, as well as prompting memories of success and enjoyment.

Teaching tip

Photographs of opportunities outside of school are also a great way to capture new and varied experiences and show the delight of exploring the community and recreational activities.

Taking it further

Use photographs for children to sequence the activity that took place and to use as prompts for them to write or talk about the experience they encountered.

Bonus idea ★

Create a rota for the children to take on the role of photographer and see how they capture the fun they are having!

It's not always easy to demonstrate progress and participation, especially if you work with children at a concrete level where objects are used and, on completion, cleared away. If there are few workbooks and written evidence, photographs provide a wealth of information for record-keeping and for sharing development with the child, parents and carers.

When children see themselves in action, the process and the engagement is accentuated. An example is food technology, where many skills are developed but the end product disappears when the product is eaten. Step-by-step photos show the child's involvement in the procedure, along with cooperation with peers, sensory experiences and active learning. Not only does the photo display remind the children of the session and the product, but it is also a genuine celebration of their part in all that was included.

It is important, however, to be very consistent on ensuring that every child is celebrated in this way. Searching for yourself and realising that you are missing is anything but motivating.

Sabotage!

'I'm trying to find ways to develop problem-solving skills, motivate the children to initiate communication and create greater independence for my class group. Any ideas?'

To develop problem solving, a certain amount of sabotage is necessary – create a situation where your children don't have exactly what they need and, rather than jumping in to intervene, wait for them to find a solution.

I can hear you thinking that this will create confusion and frustration. Sometimes, we inhibit independence and prevent the pupils from solving problems because we step in. We do a disservice if we become the personal assistant instead of the teacher! For example:

- Four children are sent to a group table but with only three chairs. I have seen this happen when a member of staff rushes to get a chair. No, no, no – stand back and give the child time to assess what is wrong and solve the problem. Use gesture and a questioning face. Ask the questions, 'What's wrong? What can you do?'

- One of the keys is to discover what it is that will motivate your pupils to make a communicative intent – to recognise that you can help them if they get your attention. Try displaying some of their favourite activities on top of a cupboard or high shelf. They can see them but cannot reach them on their own. If they can communicate verbally, help them to understand that they need to ask for the activity and you will provide it. If they require a communication system such as PECS® or an electronic device, encourage them to use this to request what is wanted. The reward will be getting the desired activity and beginning to recognise that seeking you out pays dividends.

Teaching tip

When planning a lesson, deliberately plan for a missing object or substitute a related element. For example, you have everything ready for a painting session but the brushes are not there. Encourage the pupil to recognise what is missing and find them in the labelled tray containing the brushes. No purple paint? Use this as a teaching moment to mix red and blue, allowing the children to experiment with different quantities. Through such planning, you are encouraging independence, flexibility and problem solving.

Share the good news

'My school has been trying to find new ways to celebrate the success of our children. Sometimes it seems tokenistic and we want to be genuine in the way we acknowledge success.'

Celebrations should be meaningful to staff, but it's important to ensure that the pupils are not just bystanders with little interest in what is happening 'to them'.

It is typical in schools that assemblies are used to highlight the good work of children and draw attention to the stars of the week, the best pieces of work and, in some cases, birthdays and special accomplishments. In special schools, the group size is often smaller and the length of time in assembly may be reduced. In mainstream schools, the sheer numbers in the hall and the time within the setting can be too much for children with autism. So how can you acknowledge the pupil with autism without turning the reward into a painful experience?

- Consider sharing the news with the peer group when a positive event occurs – it has more meaning when it is fresh rather than being held for the Friday assembly.
- Invite another member of staff or the headteacher into the class to offer praise in the known and familiar environment.
- Share the good news in the home–school book or through technology so that the family/carers are aware and can add to the praise at home.

While many children delight in the attention of the whole school and are happy to come to the front to receive an award and applause, this is not the case for all. It is often a time of stress for children with autism. Consider each individual and share good news in a way that brings them joy.

Bonus idea ★

Many classes have a 'star of the week' but that can be a long time to wait! Consider the 'star(s) of the day'. You may link this to the 'WOW' wall in Idea 72 and either attach a glittering star to the pupil or have an area to display the star with the child's name. Remember that you may have more than one star during the day so be prepared for this. Such a celebration is not just for curriculum success, but also for sharing, communicating, coping with stress, problem solving, etc.

Prepare to excite

'I really want to find ways to excite my pupils and help them to anticipate the fun we are going to have together, but many times they seem distracted and disinterested.'

There are times when you feel like you have created the most amazing, interesting, stimulating lesson and the response is so bland that you feel let down and discouraged.

Let's think of some ways to inspire interest and arouse enthusiasm. I have considered it a privilege over recent years to observe lessons using the Attention Autism approach. This programme supports communication, interaction, attention and learning skills in children on the autism spectrum. Using minimal language and focusing on joint attention, children are drawn into watchful participation with a sense of anticipation.

Using a multi-sensory approach also grabs the attention of children. Even introducing the day through looking at the weather can be brought to life through sound (raindrops or a clap of thunder), touch (snow, sprayed water or fanning wind) and sight (looking out of the window!). Linking objects and artefacts to stories and topics brings them alive visually and increases curiosity and wonder. Learning French in the classroom may suffice, but setting up a French café for the day and waiting on children, using appropriate phrases and serving French cuisine, will be remembered and retained for a much longer time. Remember that *you* are such an integral part of setting the scene and modelling enjoyment, through your body language, facial expression, demeanour and creative planning. You can draw your children into the wonderful world of learning – make it an adventure!

Teaching tip

The online resources provide examples of Attention Autism sessions to promote greater understanding.

Taking it further

Have a look at Attention Autism and consider how you can use this to inspire your pupils: http://best-practice. middletownautism. com/approaches-of-intervention/attention-autism/

Worthy rewards

'Is it fair to have a reward chart for my children with autism while the others in the group just get on with their work because they know what is expected of them?'

Some schools use group, team or house incentives for everyone. Many teachers have star or tick charts for everyone in the class. Creating a specific reward chart for your children who need an extra incentive, presented visually, is a reasonable adjustment to motivate them.

Ideally, a reward chart will offer an incentive that really reflects the child's interests and will motivate participation and task focus. Considering how many tokens the child should earn before the reward is offered is important. Initially, the child may only need to collect one token, increasing as the child develops the ability to sustain activities for longer periods. You should also consider whether the reward is fixed or whether it is a choice of favourite activities. For example, is Lego™ the ultimate incentive or is it perhaps a choice of Lego™, time in the quiet corner, time to draw or time on the tablet? Over time, the interests are likely to change, which needs to be reflected in the choices offered.

Managing the reward is very important. It should be time-limited, before the schedule of work is resumed. Supplementing this with some sort of timer to ensure a clear ending is always helpful and sometimes essential. Accompanying the reward time with 'First... Then...' is also helpful.

For example, Alice earns three tokens, each represented by a star. Her reward is set (colouring in) but may change over time. Leo has to earn four tokens and then has a range of choices, which may be self-selected or selected from a choice board that varies activities. As the token is earned, affix it to the spot on the chart. When the spot is covered with the token, the reward begins.

Remember, we all work for rewards. If your salary was not in the bank at the end of the month, would you keep coming to school?

Alice's Reward Chart

☆ ☆ ☆ ☆ ☆ ☆ ☆ ☆ ☆ ☆

Then Princess Colouring

Leo's Reward Chart

Work first

☐ ☐ ☐ ☐

Now I can choose

Taking it further

Rewards to motivate are as varied as the children you meet. A list of some popular examples are listed in the online resources.

Tempt me!

'Ryan rejects almost any activity I try to introduce. He has one single focus – cars – and trying to get him to participate in any areas of the curriculum is impossible.'

It is not unusual for children with autism to have single-channelled attention. They don't see the purpose in what you are trying to teach them, and without any interest in numbers and words, will continue to reject activities unless you can tempt them to see a reason.

Teaching tip

Don't fall into the trap of thinking that using Ryan's favourite topic is 'giving in' rather than a way to entice and consolidate learning. Further examples of using special interest to motivate learning and enable success are available in the online resources.

I love this challenge! When faced with a similar issue in my school, the pupil was blessed with a wonderfully creative teacher who turned his passion into a learning tool across the curriculum. So, for Ryan (in the quote above), use his passion to motivate his learning. He may not want to count cubes or objects on a worksheet but have you tried toy cars, photos of cars or car logos? Perhaps Ryan could cut out photos of cars from a motoring magazine and categorise them into makes, colours and models. Registration numbers could be used for number recognition and size comparison. Ryan could search for information on price and recommended models, leading to a report. A visit to a car dealership could be organised, with Ryan preparing questions in advance to support communication and writing a thank you letter or email to follow. The opportunities are as broad as your creative endeavours to develop them.

Another way to use Ryan's special interest is to have relevant activities and motivating resources that are immediately available when he has completed a set task – the cars become his reward and spur him on. This can be used in the 'First… Then' strategy we have discussed previously.

Affirming positive behaviour

Part 9

There's always a reason

'There are times when Aiden becomes upset and disruptive for no reason at all. It is very difficult for me and the children in his group.'

I have so often been told that there was no trigger for a child's sudden change in behaviour. Although it may not be easy to discern what caused the distress, there is _always_ a reason.

Consider this example: Aiden's teacher asked me to observe him in class, as he was having 'meltdowns' a number of times a day for no obvious reason. All went well for the first part of the morning until the children returned from playtime. Aiden joined the queue with his classmates to go to the IT room. This was his favourite part of the curriculum and he excelled at it. It was on his visual timetable. His teacher said, 'Aiden, you can't go to IT. You have your science work to finish.' You can guess what happened. As an outside observer, I knew what would happen and I understood why. From the teacher's perspective, she then reiterated to me that Aiden had a meltdown for no reason. But was this really the case?

How could this situation have been managed differently? If the timetable had inserted science work before IT, there is every possibility that Aiden would have rushed in to do this work in order to get to IT. He was not forewarned. He was right in following the schedule provided for him and the confusion was brought on because of the failure of the teacher to make his schedule concrete and predictable.

When a difficult behaviour occurs, always ask 'why?'. By analysing the situation, you can be alert to planning more appropriately, enabling the child to cope with the circumstances and be successful in managing their emotions.

A positive turn of phrase

'I often feel ignored when I have to reprimand Sophie. She acts like she doesn't understand what NO means.'

Given pupils with autism have both communication issues and literal understanding, it is important to give instructions using positive language rather than telling pupils what NOT to do.

Try turning your language around:

From this	To this
No hitting	Hands down
No running	Walking please
No pinching	Gentle hands
No swearing	Polite language

Notice the difference between the phrases above. When you tell a pupil 'no', they may not connect this with the action you are reprimanding. You are assuming that they understand what the 'no' is for. Similarly, if the pupil has receptive language difficulties, they may only hear one of the words you are using, so 'no running' becomes 'running'. That was not your intent. Saying 'stop that' does not explain *what* to stop and your command is not connected to their action.

The use of your language accompanies your demeanour, as discussed in Idea 83. If you have a raised voice, you will increase anxiety and reduce what is taken in. Your angry face will exacerbate the situation, while your calm, measured, patient, clearly spoken, positive instructions will support the child and enable them to respond more quickly and with dignity.

Everything you do contributes to the emotional wellbeing of your pupils and enables them to use the skills of positive behaviour that you are teaching them.

Teaching tip

Look at the rules in your classroom. Are they expressed in negative terms? Can they be revised to be positive? Are the rules imposed or are they generated through discussion with the children so that they both understand and have ownership of them? It's worth thinking about! Some examples of positive class rule posters and prompts for pupils are provided in the online resources.

Your demeanour

'As much as I try to stay calm when Nicky gets angry, I find that I raise my voice too and I'm sure my face reflects my annoyance.'

It's common for us to react to difficult situations by raising our voices. However, for pupils with autism, the anxiety is heightened when you respond in an annoyed and demanding way. Avoiding this is necessary to support and enable pupils with autism to calm down and recover from the situation.

Teaching tip

The prompt card is not just pulled out when a crisis begins – it is a reminder to support the child to internalise the positive behaviours.

Bear these things in mind:
- Remain calm.
- Be conscious of your body language; keep a relaxed stance with hands down.
- Speak quietly.
- Reduce your language, using key words and allowing processing time.
- Reassure the pupil by saying, 'It's okay, I'll help you' in a soothing voice.
- Offer the pupil a break – time in the quiet corner or a run to let off steam.

When the pupil has relaxed, give them time to return to a calm state before attempting to debrief. It is only then that you can try to find the source of the problem and consider coping strategies for the future. Use appropriate communication to show them other ways to manage their behaviour, e.g. well-chosen words or a visual resource such as 'Talking Mats' (see Idea 57). Support the child to develop a laminated prompt card is helpful for referral; make it credit-card size, to be carried as part of the pupil's personal toolkit.

I will remember to:
- Think first
- Ignore silly people
- Stay calm
- Tell an adult
- Stay in control
- Act sensibly

By Nicky

Recognise the signs

'I long for the time when I know my group well enough to catch behaviours before they develop into bigger issues. I am taken unawares too often!'

If only there was a little red warning light like we have in a car to alert us to something being not quite right!

Getting to know your children well, and ensuring that you have read – indeed, digested – the pupil profiles spoken of in other parts of this book, is absolutely essential. There are a wide range of warning signs that you may begin to see. For example, one child may begin to twirl her fingers in her hair, another may begin to look furtively around the room, and another may flex and intertwine his fingers. Only by knowing the unique presentation and mannerisms of the individual child can you proactively intervene and divert the pupil to avoid a negative behavioural response.

One of the children I worked with had a particular guttural sound that he made prior to losing control. He also had a happy sound, but when the former was heard, staff were immediately aware that he needed a break, a walk or a period of relaxation away from the group. Another began to rock on his chair, in danger of toppling over backwards – time for a sensory break and a few minutes on the trampette.

Once again, you need to be a detective and to be alert to idiosyncratic behaviours, sounds and movements that could result in a negative incident – or, alternatively, could be turned into a positive opportunity to reassure, offer options, pause and reflect before returning to the activity at hand.

Taking it further

Your efforts to discover the child's outward signs of anxiety will be more comprehensive if you glean information from parents/carers and colleagues who have worked with the child previously. Attempting to work in isolation will slow the process of fact-finding and impair your support for the child when most needed.

Coping strategies

'I'm trying to help Harry to recognise when he has had enough and to develop strategies to calm himself down before he loses his temper, but we are making very slow progress.'

The ultimate goal is to help children develop internalised coping strategies for managing their stress and anxiety. You, as the adult, play a key role in this.

One of my pupils responded to every frustration and perceived wrong with a total eruption. This kind of behaviour is a danger to others and frightening for all who witness it. Following such an incident, it is important to debrief in a calm and positive way. Over time, he developed his own way to cope by recognising when he was about to lose it. He would quietly ask me if he could go to the toilet, where he took a few minutes to put cold water on his face and neck. He returned when he had calmed down and would quietly tell me that he was okay. I was so proud of him!

In another setting, a mainstream child was working well on his assignment when the rest of the class became restless and loud. He looked at me, removed a stress ball from his pocket and told me he needed it for a bit. He sat quietly squeezing the ball, and after about three minutes he told me he was okay, returned it to his pocket and got on with his work in spite of the noise around him.

Pupils with autism will have to be supported to find their own unique ways to cope. Consider some of these ideas: a stretchy sensory object; malleable putty to squeeze; a short walk; a drink of water; a short time on a swing or trampette; fidget toys; time in the quiet corner snuggled in a blanket; an opportunity to spend time on an area of special interest.

A fresh start

'I know how important it is to start afresh after an incident, but it's difficult to move on without feeling tense and anticipating the next challenge.'

Overcoming a challenging incident and moving forward with confidence can be tough, particularly when there has been aggression and you feel battered and wary.

There are some key principles to consider here.

1 Deal with the incident. By this I mean that you, as an individual, need to be honest about the impact on you and seek support from understanding colleagues. Brushing off a kick, bite, hit, verbal abuse, etc., as if it doesn't matter, is *not* the way to recover from the trauma that is caused. You may need a break from the setting and this should be provided. In my experience, colleagues are very supportive and this is an essential part of a healthy school ethos.

2 Support the child. Although you may feel like the victim of an aggressive incident, there is always a reason why the child behaved in this way, and the aftermath for the child is an essential area to address. Asking the question 'why?' and exploring this with colleagues is vital. Finding the antecedent will help you to understand and will enable proactive support for the future.

3 Learn from the incident. How could this incident be avoided in the future? There are so many details to explore. Was it related to something from home that the school is not aware of? Is the child unwell in some way but cannot express this through communication? Was there too abrupt an ending to an activity without warning? Was the activity too difficult? Are there sensory issues at play?

Teaching tip

No matter what a negative behavioural episode stemmed from or resulted in, it is crucial that it is not held against the child – that it does not label the child or create negative relationships. A fresh start is essential, enabling both staff and child to move forward positively.

Taking it further

Even as adults we struggle to put a hurt or negative incident behind us. For the child, there can be a sense of worry that the strained emotion will carry on. Always start the next session or day with warmth and a demeanour that says, 'All is forgiven and we're moving on'.

Supportive approaches

'Jeremy needs some way to recognise how he is feeling – some way to understand when a situation is beginning to overwhelm him.'

Children need to begin to develop self-awareness with respect to their anxieties and resulting behaviours. It is often difficult for pupils to recognise when their anxiety is building, but as you begin to identify the precursors, you can help the pupil to develop self-awareness.

Taking it further

When things go wrong and the interventions you have developed do not seem to work effectively, take time to analyse the event with the child and to explore other strategies together. Choose a quiet, safe space and don't rush the conversation. Getting to the root of the problem will help with self-awareness and ownership of optional strategies.

Educators are very fortunate in the 21st century to have a wide range of tools available for supporting children. Here are some suggestions.

Thermometer

One tool that is often used effectively is a thermometer image, used to rate the anxiety level by colour and label – for example, from blue (calm and relaxed) to green (a little worried) and up to red (very angry – need a break).

Working with the child to help them recognise the emotion at each of these gradients, along with what causes the feeling and what aggravates the situation to move up through the scale, will help to identify when things are becoming overwhelming. Through this recognition, the child can be supported to develop strategies to stop the acceleration before it reaches red.

Social Stories™

There are many excellent books to support pupils. One of them is *There's a Volcano in my Tummy* by Éliane Whitehouse and Warwick Pudney, which helps children to understand anger. Another is *The Red Beast* by K.I. Al-Ghani, which helps children to understand how their body reacts when anger takes over. Both of these are referenced in the further reading section in the back of this book, and are great to have to hand and enjoyed by children while supporting understanding.

Physical release

Additionally, one school I visited had a 'take five punch bag', where children could request a short break to take their anxiety out on an inanimate object to release steam! For another child, it may be a time of reflection in a quiet corner. Knowing the child and the unique need is part of the challenge of enabling positive behaviour to replace aggression.

The online resources provide links to useful tools to help support positive behaviour.

Label the behaviour

'I am trying to be clear in the way I respond to behaviour. I try to ensure that Justin knows what he's done wrong, but at times I feel he has not even understood why I'm cross.'

I often hear staff reprimanding a child by using phrases such as 'Stop that' or 'Don't do that again' or 'How many times have I told you?'. Think back to what was said about inference in Idea 14. Stop what? Don't do what again? Told me what?

We are all aware that children on the autism spectrum have difficulties with communication on many different levels. While we use individualised strategies to support them in developing their communication, we must also recognise how *our* communication sometimes impedes their understanding. The onus is on us to be precise and accurate in the way we deliver messages.

For example, if a pupil repeatedly taps his pencil on the table and you tell him to stop, have you been explicit about what he needs to stop? He may stop working if his focus is on the task at hand, and not stop the tapping. In another example, rather than asking, 'How many times have I told you?', tell the child, 'I have told you to leave your comic book in your tray until your work is finished. Please put it in the tray now and remember the rule.' You are now being clear, but the instruction is explicit. Supplement it by putting a reminder on the table: 'Remember, your comic book stays in the tray until your work is finished.'

It is so easy to become exasperated and forget that the language we use can both impede understanding and cause confusion and anxiety. It's a big ask, but communicating clearly will reap dividends of understanding.

> **Bonus idea** ★
>
> Help the child to develop an understanding of your less explicit statements by asking the child what you meant. For example, when you say 'Stop that', ask the pupil what you are asking him or her to stop. If they have no idea, you should explain. By doing this, you are seeking to further develop more general communication and help your pupil to discern inference.

A shared concern

'We seem to be making real strides with supporting positive behaviour across school, but many of our families are really struggling and sometimes don't even seem to believe the progress their children are making.'

It is very common for children to behave differently at home and school, and you need to recognise this. You need to share the strategies that you are finding successful with the family/carers and work together to address common issues.

Given that children with autism struggle to generalise information, it follows that strategies that work in one context should be introduced in other contexts where the child is supported – the home, respite provision, community activities, etc.

Part of the success that schools experience is due to the clear structure and routine that constitute the school day. Through visual support and clarity of communication, the pupil knows what to expect and what comes next. By making this same strategy clear in all contexts, we enable success and acceptance of expectations.

If a visual sequence is used for changing for PE and dressing after the session but the family are struggling with these skills, share the resource, adapted as necessary. If the child is dressing independently at home and expecting staff to offer support at school, ask the family how they have achieved this.

If symbols such as 'wait' and 'quiet' are successfully used at school, introduce them to other contexts where difficulties are presented. What a bonus to have a wait symbol to use in a queue when shopping!

Taking it further

Many schools use sets of symbols attached to a lanyard or key ring on the waist. Duplicate these and make them available to parents and care staff, after explaining how this portable resource enables visual support anytime, anywhere.

Record and monitor

'Francesca has more bad days than good and seems to be out of control so often that I struggle to cope.'

I don't doubt that some pupils challenge you regularly, but it is not uncommon for us to perceive the difficult times as more frequent than they actually are. It is so important to ensure you have factual information about what is happening.

A carefully thought-through system for ensuring that incidents are logged and maintained securely is essential in providing information on individual pupils and ensuring accurate recording. Records may be handwritten in a log book, maintained either in each class or in a central location. A range of pro formas and useful websites are provided in the online resources.

Staff need to be clear on what kind of incidents are referred to; there need to be terms of reference. What constitutes a major incident that is immediately referred to senior leadership? What information is given to the parents? How is this delivered and by whom?

This information is not stagnant. It needs to be analysed on a regular basis. Is this daily? Weekly? Who has this role? How is the analysis represented and who receives this information? What trends or patterns are found? What will they lead to in terms of useful information for supporting positive behaviour management? Without this clarity, it is easy to assume that the behaviour is constant. Could it be, for example, that issues arise half an hour before dinner time? Could the behaviour be linked to low blood sugar or the odours coming from the school kitchen? Only by identifying the patterns and considering what they relate to will you begin to discern possible triggers.

Bonus idea ★

Consider forming a behaviour team in your school. Problem solving issues of challenging behaviour, analysing records and sharing good practice to improve the wellbeing of staff and pupils cannot be underestimated.

Sensory issues abound

Part 10

The game's afoot!

'Jake seemed to be agitated at different times of the day. I felt like I had to have eyes in the back of my head.'

When you begin to recognise that children on the autism spectrum may process information differently, you begin to consider their response to situations and their reaction to their surroundings in a new light. You employ specific strategies to bring children to a state of calm, alert and ready to learn and participate. Neglecting to do so fails to support the child and leads to wider issues.

It is often very difficult to identify the sensory issues that impact on a child. You need to become a detective – observing, analysing and recording situations to identify the triggers that are causing anxiety, distraction and discomfort. If the child is verbal, don't forget to begin by asking!

- Take note of WHEN you notice the change in behaviour, the anxiety, the growing distraction. This will give you a picture of whether it is linked to specific activities, commotion, noise levels, bodily needs, etc. Use sticky notes or a formal blank timetable to mark when you notice the child becoming agitated. Monitor this over a week and see whether it links to specific activities or transitions. The 'aha' moment may occur when you see that the child struggles when another group is walking down the corridor.
- Once identified, help the child to develop a coping strategy. Reassure them that, for example, the children from the other group have another room to go to but the child's class stays here right now and that's okay.

As you become more familiar with the impact of sensory issues and more alert to the signs shown by the children, you will improve your skills of detection and solve the mysteries more readily!

How it looks to me

'I tried to do an environmental audit in my classroom but I'm struggling with the adjustments I need to make to support my pupils with sensory issues.'

Making adjustments to support sensory issues is a common problem, and there are some things that are difficult to change. Oh, for a purpose-built school where lighting has been specifically designed and window shades reduce glare! Most schools were built long before we recognised the sensory needs of children, and it takes creative adaptations to manage the frustrations that arise.

Of course, lighting is far from the only distraction in classrooms. Primary schools are known for the quality of display, magnificent mobiles, trails of words and numbers, and bunting to die for. While these are stimulating for many children, they can be overwhelming for your children on the autism spectrum, and a measure of compromise in meeting the needs of *all* is essential. Here are some tips to try:

- Reduce the number of things dangling from the ceiling.
- Limit the number of displays.
- Move a display board outside of the classroom and into the corridor.
- Have some individual word banks and maths facts for pupils to use at their desks, rather than putting everything on the wall.
- Create an area in the classroom that is low arousal (see Idea 27).
- Develop a work station facing a blank wall where distraction is minimised (see Idea 26).
- Provide window blinds that reduce sunlight and glare.
- Replace flickering fluorescent lights if possible.
- Optimise the use of natural light.
- Create an atmosphere of semi-darkness for special story times and relaxation.

Taking it further

Investigate fluorescent light filters, available through Educational Insights: https://www. educationalinsights.com/. Further useful resources and website links are provided in the online resources.

Bonus idea ★

Start the year with a minimalist approach and build up gradually, slowly introducing colour and display.

What is that noise?

'Everything will be fine and then, all of a sudden, he screams and dives under the table, covering his ears!'

When a child suddenly cries out or dives for cover, it can be alarming and frightening for both staff and children. Finding the reason behind the action is often illusive and requires your best skills of detection to solve the dilemma.

The situation described above was happening several times a day, and the teacher invited me to observe in the classroom to see whether I could discern what was happening. I sat, watched, listened, observed and witnessed the concern. I had no idea why. I sat, watched, listened, observed and witnessed it again. The third time I had an inkling and tested it out. The fourth time, I was sure.

Now this is what I mean by detective work. I finally picked up on the sound of a very squeaky door outside the classroom in the corridor. Although it was audible to me, listening very carefully, no one in the busy classroom was attuned to it at all – no one apart from the boy whose ears were hurting every time the door opened and closed. Solution: oil the hinges. Problem solved! But without an extra pair of eyes and ears, it would have continued to go unnoticed.

Watch for:

- hands covering ears
- retreating from a situation
- distraction and furtive glances.

Once you recognise a trigger, be creative about helping the child to cope. Attempt to explain the sound and reduce the fear that it may cause. For example, show him the squeaky door. Could he help hold the oil can?

Bonus idea ★

Provide ear defenders for the child's use. By muffling sound input, there is a better chance of calm and control. For some, favoured music at appropriate times in the day can be beneficial.

I can feel it

'Anne pulls her hands back as soon as I introduce any tactile materials. She gets really upset if anyone touches her unexpectedly.'

The girl in the quote, Anne, is clearly sensitive to touch — tactile-defensive on two fronts. Supporting her by trying to desensitise her may be a slow process but helpful in the long run.

To help Anne begin to explore materials, try to make it fun. Let her squirt shaving foam on you or on a face template to make a beard, or squirt cream on a dessert. Exaggerate the fun of touching and try to draw her into the experience. Engage her through food technology sessions where many different ingredients are used, and encourage feeling and describing.

When a touch feels like an aggressive act, it can be frightening. Children bump into each other often and just take it in their stride, but if it is misinterpreted as aggressive and deliberate, issues arise. If Anne gets upset, use a 'teaching moment' to explain what happened and reassure her that it was just an accident. Use role play to help Anne see the difference between a bump and a thump. Use puppets to tell a story to show incidents relating to misunderstanding.

Common tactile sensory issues to watch out for include:

- labels in clothing causing extreme discomfort
- failure to recognise the extremes of hot and cold and needing to be reminded to dress appropriately for the weather
- discomfort of light touch, while deep massage may be welcomed.

Teaching tip

Don't expect overnight success. It can be a slow and steady process to build up confidence and the courage to investigate different materials.

Taking it further

Seek the advice of a specialist in sensory integration.

Bonus idea ★

Train up a member of staff in sensory integration to take the role of sensory lead in your school — establish a Sensory Detective Agency!

Oh that smell!

'I noticed that Chris became unsettled and distracted as it got closer to dinner time but just couldn't figure out why.'

You may assume that a child who becomes unsettled near dinner time is hungry and has low blood sugar. Let's think about other reasons. As dinner time draws closer, the odours from the kitchen become stronger. For a child with hyper-sensory olfactory sense, this can be a real distraction, especially if it triggers distaste!

Teaching tip

Liaise with parents/carers to understand both pleasant and intolerable odours. Have they found ways to build tolerance that can support consistency in school?

Bonus idea ★

Develop some 'sniffing' activities for the children to guess the product and give opinions about whether they like or dislike it. Some schools introduce an 'Aroma of the Week' to expose children to various scents. Worth a try!

There are so many distractions and reactions through smell. Recognising this can help you to understand the discomfort of children you are working with. For example, a child may push you away if they dislike the smell of your perfume, soap, shampoo or breath; they might sniff you if they like these smells. A child might refuse to go to the school toilet if there is an overwhelming odour, or reject materials such as plasticine because of the smell.

Some of these things are difficult to change, as the elimination of some odours is virtually impossible. Once recognised, you may choose to try to avoid both personal products and resources or to try new brands to see whether they are more acceptable. Teaching tolerance is important, as is reducing the amount of time using a material. You might try opting for coloured pencils rather than felts or paints, for example. Generally, try to be flexible yourself and to help the child to understand the need to be flexible and to build up tolerance.

Suggested ideas for activities and resources are provided in the online resources.

The trouble with tasting

'We are very concerned about Patrick's limited diet. It seems so unhealthy.'

It is quite common for children with autism to have unusual diets. This may be related to rejecting the texture, taste or colour of food. It's not uncommon for a child to be able to discern between two brands of the same food and reject the one that is not used in the home.

What is the school's responsibility in supporting or influencing a child's nutrition? Because we are concerned about the *whole* child, we should work alongside parents/carers and, in some cases, a dietician, to widen options and introduce a healthy diet. Forcing the child to eat foods that are rejected is unlikely to be a way forward!

I have previously worked with a child whose entire daily intake was composed of crisps and chocolate buttons. That was it – full stop! Through home and school working together, he was first introduced to tolerating a dinner plate with a small portion of food placed on the table at arm's length. When this was accepted, it was gradually moved closer. The next step was for him to put one piece of food on a fork; next was to sniff the piece, then to touch it with his tongue and, eventually, to taste. The first success was a slice of apple, and apples were added to his diet – a wonderful success! But, importantly, it took time. It took months to reach this point and then to extend his diet to accept a wider range of food from healthy options.

Teaching tip

Always work closely with the child's family/carers to understand the full picture of the dietary issues. The school is only one part of a much wider picture and needs to work in tandem with others caring for the child.

Bonus idea ★

Take advantage of the wonderful ideas for children's food options on Pinterest, where fruits and vegetables can be turned into many shapes to entice children. Respond to hypo and hyper taste buds, offering bland and spicy options.

The way my body moves

'Susan often bumped into things and fell over. She pressed so hard with pencils that they broke and sometimes she complained that things were too heavy.'

You need to understand the sensory challenges some children face. Rather than scolding, look for reasons and offer interventions to support.

Taking it further

A wide range of equipment and resources are available, including wobble cushions, ball chairs, weighted blankets and vests, weighted backpacks, various swings, climbing frames, balance beams and exercise balls. Explore the range by searching for sensory resources online.

Many of us would only recognise five senses – smell, taste, touch, sound and sight. But there are more! Understanding the proprioceptive and vestibular senses answers more of the questions that our children raise.

Proprioceptive refers to the stimuli related to position and movement of the body, effort, force and heaviness. One child who always wore long sleeves with a buttoned cuff explained that it was the only way he knew where his arms ended. Susan may benefit from 'heavy work' – pushing and pulling, lifting and climbing – linked to tasks such as using gardening tools, wiping tables and carrying shopping bags.

Vestibular relates to balance, stability and movement – the sense of body rotation and gravitation arising from the inner ear. Your pupils may be anxious to take their feet off the ground, find spaces too big or too small, or fear stepping through doorways or sitting on the toilet. A range of basic movements support development, including swinging, jumping, rolling, spinning and climbing.

Ask for expert advice from an occupational therapist specialising in sensory integration, and ensure that you follow guidelines for the appropriate use of activities and resources. Further information and practical support is provided in the online resources.

Sensory diets

'When I first heard the term "sensory diet", I thought it was a range of menu choices to encourage variety in eating.'

A sensory diet is NOT what you plan for lunch, but a range of activities and interventions that support the child when discomfort or sensory overload begin to raise anxieties and erode opportunities for learning and enjoying the school routine.

A sensory diet to *proactively* avert anxiety enables the child to access appropriate breaks and resources throughout the day. This is not a one-size-fits-all tool but an individualised, bespoke menu planned specifically for the child.

- For one child, you may offer a few minutes to curl up in a blanket in the quiet corner and listen to soft music through headphones.
- For another, you may have a few minutes of running in the playground and a set number of bounces on the trampette.
- For others, this may be manipulating a fidget toy or sticky tack, swinging in the playground or sensory room, or a small healthy snack.

Short burst: These short breaks help the child to reduce anxiety, calm down and be directed back to the task at hand. It may be necessary to use a timer or to use 'First... Then' to make it very clear that the break has ended.

Directed or choice: By using a choice board of appropriate activities and resources, you can empower the child to choose their preferred option rather than imposing something on the child.

Coping strategies: Making sensory diets available *before* stress overtakes a situation enables the pupil to maintain positive behaviour and to develop individual coping strategies that can be generalised to other contexts.

Taking it further

Share the successful strategies you have discovered with others who support the child, such as parents/carers, respite facilities, other staff across school and those supporting outside of school hours.

Bonus idea ★

Access the online resources for this book for practical examples of sensory diets and how they can be used throughout the day.

Start the day right

'There were times when I was so defeated by the start of the day in the classroom that I didn't know how any of us would be ready for teaching and learning.'

We would all like to have a calm, smooth start to our day, and many households fail to achieve such bliss. Add to this the challenge of transitions, the bombardment of sensory overload and, in many cases, a long journey to school, and the scene is set for a stormy start!

Teaching tip

A range of suggestions to succeed in starting the day right can be found in the online resources.

Bonus idea ★

I have been in a number of schools where this calming technique is used to great effect, by using visuals to encourage the children to breathe in and exhale as part of relaxing at designated times of the day. Encourage children to 'smell the flowers' and 'blow out the candles', with corresponding pictures. This can be repeated several times, with both staff and children participating – oh the calm!

For many children with autism, the transition from home to school is stressful, and by providing ways to release tension and sensitively move into the routine of the day, we can enable a positive start and lay the foundation for the daily routine.

Welcome the children into a calm setting – quiet music, minimal language, smiles and orderly routine all contribute to relaxing both staff and children. The consistent atmosphere you establish will make it possible for the children to predict their transition into school and feel secure. Using appropriate visuals will reinforce the daily routine and provide clarity.

Seek the advice of an occupational therapist who specialises in sensory integration to support individual programmes and train staff to develop:

- **Sensory circuits:** For children who have been travelling a distance to school, having a time of structured exercise and movement sets them up for the start of the school day.
- **Calming:** Finish the circuit time with a session of calm relaxation.
- **Be alert and ready for learning:** Supporting the child to be in the right pace for learning, not too lethargic nor too high spirited.
- For further advice, look up 'The Alert Programme' and its online resources.

A bank of ideas

'I went on a couple of sensory courses and began to realise that some of the ideas weren't actually rocket science. I invited some colleagues to join me in developing a resource bank for my school. It really has paid off.'

Sensory issues really do abound, but when staff work together to share good practice and develop a bank of ideas, it enables everyone to have strategies and resources readily available.

When developing your idea bank, call upon the professionals who support your school and the parents/carers who know their child so well. List activities and resources that support the seven sensory areas. Seek the support of a sensory integration specialist.

- Motivate interested colleagues to work with you. Tackle one area at a time by sharing ideas and investigating further through books and online sources.
- Put the resource bank together in an attractive and easily accessible format with text and diagrams, as well as ensuring that the resources listed are available in your school. Have some samples of concrete ideas, such as visuals and choice boards. (You could store this in paper copy or on a shared drive, but ensure that it is accessible and regularly updated.)

Launch the resource bank to all staff, ensuring that each has an awareness of sensory issues and how they can be supported. Help them to understand that each child presents with autism differently and that new ideas will be added when new situations and solutions arise. Encourage colleagues to see the resource as a working tool rather than a file on a shelf. Some ideas to help you on your way with your bank of ideas can be found in the online resources.

Taking it further

Make links with other schools in your area where sensory needs are being addressed. Start a focus group of interested colleagues, to share case studies of children in different contexts and share solutions together.

Further reading

A wealth of information is available to further your understanding of pupils on the autistic spectrum. The following is a partial list of recommended reading and websites and each, in turn, will lead you to further links. Enjoy your journey of investigation and learning.

Books

Adams, S. (2008) *A Book About What Autism Can Be Like*. London: Jessica Kingsley Publishers.

Atwood, T. (1997) *Asperger's Syndrome: A Guide for Parents and Professionals*. London: Jessica Kingsley Publishers.

Barton, M. (2011) *It's Raining Cats and Dogs: An Autism Spectrum Guide to the Confusing World of Idioms, Metaphors and Everyday Expressions*. London: Jessica Kingsley Publishers.

Bates, H. and Li, E. (2016) *A Girl Like Tilly: Growing up with Autism*. London: Jessica Kingsley Publishers.

Bogdashina, O. (2005) *Theory of Mind and the Triad of Perspectives on Autism and Asperger Syndrome*. London: Jessica Kingsley Publishers.

Bogdashina, O. (2016) *Sensory Perceptual Issues in Autism and Asperger Syndrome (2nd edn)*. London: Jessica Kingsley Publishers.

Brukner, L. and Liebstein, L. (2018) *Simple Things to Get kids Self-Regulating in School*. London: Jessica Kingsley Publishers.

Coyne, P., Klagge, M. and Nyberg, C. (2016) *Developing Leisure Time Skills for People with Autism Spectrum Disorders*. Arlington, TX: Future Horizons Incorporated.

Elder, J. (2005) *Different Like Me, My Book of Autism Heroes*. London: Jessica Kingsley Publishers.

Elvén, H. B. (2010) *No Fighting, No Biting, No Screaming*. London: Jessica Kingsley Publishers.

Grandin, T. (2006) *Thinking in Pictures (2nd edn)*. New York: Vintage Books.

Gray, C. (2010) *The New Social Story Book (revised edn)*. Arlington, TX: Future Horizons Incorporated.

Harvey, C. (2018) *Difference Not Disorder*. London: Jessica Kingsley Publishers.

Higashida, N. (2007) *The Reason I Jump*. New York: Penguin Random House.

James, M. (2018) *Forest Schools and Autism: A Practical Guide*. London: Jessica Kingsley Publishers.

Mackenzie, H. (2008) *Reaching and Teaching the Child with Autism Spectrum Disorder.* London: Jessica Kingsley Publishers.

Mielnick, M. (2017) *Understanding Sensory Processing Disorders in Children.* London: Jessica Kingsley Publishers.

Moyes, R. (2012) *Visual Techniques for Developing Social Skills.* Arlington, TX: Future Horizons Incorporated.

Notbohm, E. (2007) *Ten Things Every Child with Autism Wishes You Knew (2nd edn).* Arlington, TX: Future Horizons Incorporated.

Pudney, W. and Whitehouse, E. (1998) *There's a Volcano in my Tummy.* BC, Canada: New Society Publishers.

Sainsbury, C. (2000) *Martian in the Playground.* Bristol: Lucky Duck Publishing Ltd.

Seach, D., Lloyd, M. and Preston, M. (2002) *Supporting Children with Autism in Mainstream Schools.* London: Bloomsbury.

Shawl, J. (2014) *The Conversation Train.* London: Jessica Kingsley Publishers.

Shawl, J. (2017) *The ASD and Me Picture Book.* London: Jessica Kingsley Publishers.

Shawl, J. (2017) *The ASD Feel Better Book.* London: Jessica Kingsley Publishers.

Timmins, S. (2016) *Successful Social Stories™ for Young Children with Autism.* London: Jessica Kingsley Publishers.

Whitcomb Marsh, W. (2018) *The ABCs of Autism in the Classroom.* Arlington, TX: Future Horizons Incorporated.

Williams, C. and Wright, B. (2016) *A Guide to Writing Social Stories™.* London: Jessica Kingsley Publishers.

Resources and books for supporting and reading with children

Adams, S. (2008) *A Book About What Autism Can Be Like.* London: Jessica Kingsley Publishers.

Al-Ghani, K. (2008) *The Red Beast.* London: Jessica Kingsley Publishers.

Al-Ghani, K. (2017) *Wilson Wallaby Can't Stop.* London: Jessica Kingsley Publishers.

Brady, L. J., Gonzalez, A. X., Zawadzki, M. and Presley, C. (2012) *Speak, Move, Play and Learn with Children on the Autism Spectrum.* London: Jessica Kingsley Publishers.

Coelho, A. (2017) *Sometimes Noise is Big.* London: Jessica Kingsley Publishers.

Harvey, N. (2018) *Mindful Little Yogis.* London: Jessica Kingsley Publishers.

LeGoff, D. (2017) *How Lego®-Based Therapy for Autism Works.* London: Jessica Kingsley Publishers.

Manasco, H. (2012) *An Exceptional Children's Guide to Touch.* London: Jessica Kingsley Publishers.

Mehrabian, A. (1971) *Silent Messages*. Wadsworth Publishing Co., University of Michigan.

Miller, A. (2018) *All About Me*. London: Jessica Kingsley Publishers.

O'Sullivan, N. (2014) *I'll Tell You Why I Can't Wear Those Clothes!* London: Jessica Kingsley Publishers.

Pimley, L. and Bowen, M. (2008) *The Autism Inclusion Toolkit*. London: Sage Publications.

Porter, J. (2011) *Autism and Reading Comprehension*. Arlington, TX: Future Horizons Incorporated.

Rawlins, A. (2017) *Is It OK to Ask Questions About Autism?* London: Jessica Kingsley Publishers.

Rudolph, S. (2015) *All My Stripes: A Story for Children with Autism*. USA: American Psychological Association.

Whelan Banks, J. (2008) *Liam Wins the Game, Sometimes*. London: Jessica Kingsley Publishers.

Whelan Banks, J. (2008) *Liam Says 'Hi'*. London: Jessica Kingsley Publishers.

Zysk, V. (2018) *Manners Matter*. Arlington, USA: Future Horizons Incorporated.

Useful information

- National Autistic Society – https://www.autism.org.uk/
- PECS – the Picture Exchange Communication System® – http://www.pecs.org.uk/
- Social Stories™ – https://www.thegraycenter.org/
- TEACCH – Treatment and Education of Autistic and Related Communication Handicapped Children – https://teacch.com/